COUNTRY
—KITCHENS—

COUNTRY
KITCHENS

JOCASTA INNES
PHOTOGRAPHY BY JAMES MERRELL

UNIVERSE

COUNTRY KITCHENS
Jocasta Innes
Photography by James Merrell

First paperback edition published in the United States of America
in 1996 by UNIVERSE PUBLISHING
A Division of Rizzoli International Publications, Inc.
300 Park Avenue South
New York, NY 10010

Edited and designed by Mitchell Beazley
an imprint of Octopus Publishing Group Limited.

Senior Executive Art Editor **Jacqui Small**
Executive Editor **Judith More**
Assistant Art Editor **Trinity Fry**
Recipe Editor **Jenni Fleetwood**
Home Economists **Nigel Slater, Carol Handslip**
Editorial Assistants **Rachel Addis, Halley Cohen**
Production **Ted Timberlake**

Library of Congress Catalog Card Number: 96-60503
ISBN 0-7893-0069-9

The publishers have made every effort to ensure that all instructions
given in this book are accurate and safe, but they cannot accept
liability for any resulting injury, damage or loss to either person or
property whether direct or consequential and howsoever arising.
The authors and publishers will be grateful for any information which
will assist them in keeping future editions up to date.

Typeset in Baskerville No2, 11.5/16pt.
by Litho Link, Welshpool, Powys, Wales
Colour reproduction by Scantrans Pte Ltd, Singapore
Produced by Toppan Printing Co., (H.K.) Ltd.
Printed and bound in China
2002 2003 2004/10 9 8 7 6 5 4 3 2

CONTENTS

FOREWORD

What makes a kitchen feel countrified is never the simple fact of its being located in the countryside. Neither of the two country kitchens I have had, one past, one present, are anywhere near as countrified as the one in my London house. What to me gives any kitchen a countrified atmosphere is its absolute centrality to the life of the household. People – visitors as much as residents – gravitate there.

This is partly a question of size. My London kitchen is big; we have managed to squeeze 20 or so people around the long scrubbed table. Also, it has such rustic accoutrements as a brick floor, a solid-fuel range, a dresser, a wooden drainer and a porcelain sink. No one would describe my kitchen as smart or stylish, but it is mellow and comforting and real, as are so many of the kitchens visited in this book. There is a reaction in decoration, as in food, against primping things up. All of a sudden, naturalness is more interesting, more humane, than perfection. Fashion is not absent, but for every stack of chic black and silver pans, you will see many more humble jumbles of beloved old crocks crazed and blackened with use, wooden spoons smoothed as sea shells, little jars and tins that have taken on an indispensable character – this one for china tea, that for peppercorns, a lidless sardine dish for butter . . . . .

Real kitchens are full of mysteries to perplex the first-time visitor. But not for long – I have a strong feeling that if I were put down in any one of the homes shown in these pages, I would find my way around in just a few minutes. Partly, it is true, because there is a sensible policy of keeping a good part of the *batterie de cuisine* on view, but also because instinct and tradition have overtaken theory in the arrangement of these kitchens, and this is a map that anyone who cooks can read.

Right: This room adheres to two classic tenets of the country kitchen by featuring a table where food is prepared and eaten and an array of shelving that displays essentials within easy reach.

Capacious dressers (actually new and purpose-built, but disguised by a clever paint job), a well-worn central table and a chunky butcher's block evoke the atmosphere of a traditional 19th-century country house kitchen. In fact, this attractive room, with its softly colourwashed walls, is right in the heart of London. Unusual accessories – a Venetian glass light fitting, tole canisters, a roll-top bread bin – contribute to the sophisticatedly simple effect.

—KITCHEN—
STYLE

This chapter examines the basic design decisions you should make before you install a country kitchen. You could choose a built-in or an unstructured style – matching cupboards or a mixture of freestanding furniture. Or you could opt for a compromise arrangement that gives an unstructured look without losing the built-in organization of the modern kitchen.

Deciding on the type of installation is only a beginning; the next stage – although it is often bound up with the first – is to select the materials for your cupboards. Would you prefer the solid beauty of natural wooden cupboards or would one of the many styles of painted kitchen furniture suit your needs best? Whether your kitchen – or your budget – is large or small, you will find ample inspiration in the following pages.

MIX OR MATCH

Until just a few years ago a co-ordinating, built-in kitchen was everyone's ideal. Cooks hankered after an intensely planned run of cupboards that presented an unbroken – no cracks for dirt to hide in – expanse of ergonomically sound storage and working surface. Kitchens that feature this high degree of organization of space are one of the legacies of the Modern Movement; a design response to a brave new world where gadgets replaced servants and cooking was represented as a chore to be dealt with quickly and efficiently.

This approach to kitchen design has by no means been invalidated and today a built-in kitchen is still far and away the most popular type. However, the co-ordinated look does not answer everyone's idea of how a kitchen should appear or function. As a response to this, there has been a revival of interest in apparently unstructured kitchens. Several manufacturers have produced styles of furniture designed to give the air of an old-fashioned, countrified kitchen which "just growed" over generations. Ironically, most of

The period-style room shown here is an excellent example of how furniture of different periods, countries and finishes can mix happily together and create a kitchen with the enviable "just growed together" look. In fact, much care has gone into details like the green painted door (below left) that picks up the colour of an old armoire standing beside it (below right). Note the handsome effect of tiles inset in a brick floor, making a "rug" which fits under the polished refectory table and companionable cluster of unmatched wooden chairs. The rustic chandelier uses candlepower only and looks completely at home hooked to a stout oak beam. Aside from the beams, which are original, the entire room is a brilliant fabrication, using antiques, newly built furniture, well-chosen accessories and lots of textures to suggest centuries of use.

the commercially produced "unfitted" kitchens cost substantially more than the built-in variety. On the other hand, once you grasp the basic requirements of the look and work out how to smuggle in gadgetry and equipment without losing the unstructured effect, there is no reason why you can't, as it were, "grow" your own. Simply combine junk, secondhand and reproduction pieces to come up with what is, after all, an updated version of the sort of kitchen that was prevalent up until the 20th century.

Before arriving at a decision over which type of kitchen to choose – built-in or freestanding – you should consider the advantages and disadvantages of both. The space available, existing equipment (supposing you are not starting from scratch), the way that you like to cook and eat and, ultimately, your own temperament are all part of the equation.

Built-in kitchens are probably the most rational solution to small, cramped quarters that have structural problems such as lack of daylight, irregular shapes or odd floor levels. Primitive, unstructured old cottage kitchens,

with their stone sinks and higgledy-piggledy shelving, have great charm. But they are definitely not labour-saving – you need plenty of time and a well-established routine to cope with limited, ad-hoc equipment. Butler sinks and teak draining boards, for instance, demand constant bleaching, scrubbing and sterilizing, whereas stainless steel requires only a quick wipe.

I would cope with the "too small to swing a cat" situation by running floorstanding cupboards along two or three walls and incorporating the refrigerator, dishwasher and so on behind concealing doors. Choose doors made from natural wood or finished with a special paint effect, rather than in laminate. Such finishes look friendly rather than clinical, especially if you can afford work surfaces made from natural materials – tiles, slate, zinc or wood. Step away from the conventional "en-suite" wall-mounted cupboards by choosing glazed doors and painting the insides a strong, rich contrast colour, peasant style. Or opt for some open storage – hanging shelves, overhead racks for pots and pans, plenty of knives on magnetic racks and jars stuffed with wooden spoons.

My own experience of cooking in all sorts of situations for umpteen people is that having much-used equipment to hand, and visible, saves time and thought. Most basic utensils are handsome things anyway, much too pleasing to hide in drawers. Having said that, drawers are a necessity, although often they are skimped on in commercial furniture because they are complicated to make. One stack of fairly deep, smooth-running drawers is not too many to hold cutlery, dishtowels, cookie cutters, rolling pins, barbecue skewers and all the other flotsam and jetsam which needs to lie flat but be easily accessible.

A lot of the elaborate and ingenious ideas incorporated in modern kitchen furniture are less wonderful in practice than they sound in a brochure. Carousel or lazy susan fittings for corners can be virtually inaccessible if space is tight, while open shelves designed to fit at the end of a run of wall or base cupboards are more often than not an invitation to unsightly clutter, rather than a home for a beautiful fruit basket or pottery paté dish. More useful are the sort of wall cupboards which come down to meet the work counter, so that you don't have to keep lifting hefty gadgets like mixers up and down, and extra

A brand-new kitchen extension to an 18th century country house cleverly combines traditional features – barn-style roof, brick paving, elegant windows – with modern purpose-built furnishings. Everything has been planned with great care. The elegantly crafted Smallbone cupboards and dressers have ample drawers, the work surfaces include slots for kitchen knives and inset marble slabs for rolling pastry. The fireplace acts as a room divider, as well as a source of light and heat, separating the eating end of the room, below, from the work area, left.

work surfaces which slide out from under the main work counter and can be used as an additional chopping board or as a place to stand things when cooking flat out.

Eating in the kitchen, rather than in a formal dining room, adds a country flavour to meal times. Even the smallest kitchen usually has space for a table and chairs or stools, although this may mean that you have to put the washing machine in the bathroom, garage or basement. Perching on stools side-by-side at a worktop counter is better than nothing, but generally looks a little too fast-food for a country kitchen.

The final point in favour of a built-in kitchen is that it is a great help to the temperamentally disorganized. There is something calming and mind-clearing about "a place for everything and everything in its place." In a busy life this more than compensates for a certain loss of hominess.

A homey style is the whole aim of the unstructured kitchen. Family room first and kitchen second is the effect that should be created. The key elements are pieces of furniture – a large, central table, a substantial freestanding dresser or armoire, even an easy chair or two – while the working area is discreetly tucked away or disguised.

The style of commercially available unstructured kitchens hovers somewhere between Provençal, Santa Fe and Tuscan in its inspiration, with much use of solid, chunky wood, bright tiles and baskets for storage. Many feature islands – an effective ruse for building in a lot of practical, up-to-date equipment unobtrusively. In a large room a bank of built-in cupboards (no need to be too literal about this, it's an unstructured look you are after) might run across one end, with the island standing centrally a couple of yards/metres in front. The island can be as simple as an outsize butcher's block mounted on a frame – a

place to chop, mix and dish up – or it can be a cupboard and counter complex housing anything from a mini-sink to a griddle plate or a marble slab for pastry-making.

Where there is space to take it, a well-thought-out island is a real boon. It is effectively a second kitchen table, but at a better working height and with space to stash trash containers and quite large gadgets out of sight below. Because it depends on re-routing services like power, gas and water to the middle of the floor, installing an island is best done when building a kitchen from scratch or, at the very least, putting in a new floor. Make sure that the island has good overhead lighting; preferably a fixture that can be raised and lowered.

What really marks off the unstructured look from the built-in sort is the use of freestanding furniture. A big old armoire, painted or polished, is an excellent choice. This type of cupboard is useful as well as decorative – you can store table linen, special china and glass and homemade preserves in it. If more storage is needed a dresser – or two or three – is an obvious solution. A more unusual one is a secondhand shop fitment, preferably with glazed doors.

A capacious table is also important in an unstructured kitchen. The design should be sturdy and simple – more farmhouse refectory than shining mahogany. Oak, walnut, scrubbed pine or deal all have the right look. But deal, like a lot of good things, needs daily maintenance to keep it invitingly blanched and unspotted. Use a scrubbing brush and a proprietary cleaner with a built-in bleach and work with the grain. Chairs don't have to match, but they should be in the same style family – sturdy, and maybe rush- or cane-seated for lightness. Where space allows, an armchair or two or a squashy sofa where people can chat to the cook will add to the cosy look.

This sunshine yellow Hollywood kitchen is essentially a classic modern built-in design, countrified by the use of natural materials – wood counters, rush-seated chairs – and country accessories. Restaurant owner Richard Irving dries home-grown red chillies to make an original frieze around the walls. Great spiky bundles of rosemary and buckets full of flowers add to the air of generous natural profusion. More colour and pattern is introduced with chintz and toile de Jouy *fabrics and blue and white china.*

Right: At first glance, this kitchen bears very little resemblance to a modern kitchen. But built-in dressers like the wall-sized example shown here were the earliest type of custom kitchen furniture. The period mood is continued by slotting an old-fashioned butler's sink into a purpose-built cupboard, while the original fireplace swallows up the Aga.

Top left: Built-in furniture is the best solution for tiny kitchens like this cottage example, where space is very limited.

Middle left: Period features like wall-hung shelving are combined with a very practical, well-planned modern workspace, complete with dishwasher and oven slotted into the front of fitted cupboards in old pine.

Bottom left: In a traditional kitchen sloping whitewashed rafters bristle with hooks for tidying away pots, pans and baskets, freeing counterspace.

PAINTED
—KITCHENS—

Paint is the cheapest form of decoration, especially if you apply it yourself. Specialist paint manufacturers carry ranges based on period hues, such as yellow ochres and red oxides, ultramarine blues and Brunswick green. Although authentic in appearance, these paints are often made to modern formulations for improved drying speed and quick coverage. The substantial colours are best aged with a final coat of varnish that has been "dirtied" with raw umber.

You can learn a great deal about traditional

My tiny galley kitchen, sliced off the immense central space of a converted chapel, seemed to call for a dramatic colour scheme. I chose rich dark hues that might have been used in a 19th century church interior. The stencils are on-going – I add another row when rain keeps me in at the weekend.

It makes every kind of sense for potters Hinchcliffe and Barber to line kitchen walls with their own work, especially when the tiles are as attractive as these. The blue and green of the animal motifs are picked up throughout the room – deep green on general wood-work and fireplaces, blues for crockery (all their own make, naturally) and cotton prints, and a glorious in-between shade for the run of built-in cupboards along the back wall.

paint styles by simply studying a piece of period painted furniture carefully, still more by trying to copy it. On the whole, a peasant piece is lifeless unless further enriched and embellished by traditional motifs, carried out in strong contrasting colours and finished off with little decorative flicks and flourishes in white or black.

But if fluent brushwork and bold adaptation is not your strong suit, there are easier ways to create richly decorated surfaces. Stencils are the best-known tool. Today, they can be found in a very wide range of designs, from demure small-scale motifs to rampant floral pieces or splendid baskets overflowing with harvests of fruit and flowers. If you take a basic cupboard, place large motifs in the middle of its panels and then add stencilled borders, you will have the makings of a traditional-looking painted piece. Stencils have a sort of primness which is part of their charm. If you prefer a loose, freestyle approach, look for the new "painting patterns" which illustrate step-by-step how to trace off and colour in motifs from different periods and national styles. Painting by numbers, maybe, but you will find these satisfying to do and surprisingly effective.

The sort of kitchen furniture that can be painted ranges from chunky old pieces run to earth in antique or junk shops or markets to an increasingly varied and stylish range of reproduction items specifically designed for painting. Most of these are constructed of MDF (medium-density fibreboard), inexpensive whitewood, deal or ply, and a good painted finish is the making of them.

Easy-to-use matte water-based paints chosen from standard paint charts are replacing slow-drying oil-based paints and glazes as a finish for furniture as well as walls. They have the advantage of "dry" texture, strong colours and excellent coverage. To avoid a plastic effect either distress or sponge on different coloured layers for texture, or add bold stencilled motifs, and finish with a tinted matte varnish to protect the surface.

Strongly decorated pieces, whatever their size, look best against yet more strong colour and/or pattern. To isolate items like a brilliantly floral clock case or dresser against plain white walls will diminish them; they become garish. Originally, painted furniture was set off by painted or rough wooden walls, or stencilled surfaces. Colourful dressers will look even handsomer if the plates, cups or whatever they are filled with are in bright

Left: You can easily achieve the effect of an old-fashioned dresser by topping a long run of built-in cupboards with open shelving. Paint them both in the same shade.

Above: The grass-green painted woodwork is a rich contrast to the terracotta-tiled floor. The smaller door to the right of the passageway once led to a below-stairs glory hole. This has been converted into a shallow store cupboard, with the refrigerator slotted into the remaining space beyond.

colours too. But make sure that you know where to draw the line; don't have everything in the kitchen painted with hearts and flowers or acanthus scrolls. Save these motifs for one big piece and use simple combing or vinegar-graining elsewhere.

Paint is a simple and inexpensive way to produce a unique custom result. For example, you can combine two or more rich colours such as red or green with blue on cabinets to co-ordinate – or contrast – with the walls, or you can use a special grained paint effect on softwood or MDF surfaces to simulate the appearance of a more costly hardwood like oak or cherry. Before you rip out ugly cabinets consider whether, instead, it is possible to transform them with the judicious use of paint.

If you have a dull run of kitchen cupboards it is tempting to decorate them with elaborate patterns. However, on the whole these sort of cabinets look best with an understated finish. Try sponging or colourwashing them in a single gentle colour such as duck egg blue or palest terracotta. Alternatively, use a soft-coloured glaze to apply the ubiquitous dragged finished over a white ground.

Paint doesn't have to be restricted to the outsides of cabinets – glazed cupboards or dressers look doubly delightful if the insides are painted in a soft colour.

For anyone setting up home on a limited budget the great attraction of the hand-painted style of kitchen is that it allows you to "lose" ugly cupboards or graceless items by painting them in one colour, while on the other hand enabling you to exploit colour, pattern and texture to feature the pieces that you are proud of. If you take up your paint-brush and paints to blend old with new, reproduction with junk, you will finish up with an inexpensive kitchen that is as unique and individual as the costliest custom-designed scheme.

WOODEN
——KITCHENS——

*Right and above: This simple
California kitchen is furnished with
handsome custom-made furniture. The
wood was grit-blasted, then dry-
brushed with palest matte gray paint
to bring out its rugged, blanched
appearance. White-stained adobe tiles
tone with the wood.*

Wood and country kitchens are natural partners. Unadorned wooden cupboards can be cosily rustic, like the New England kitchen shown on page 47, while the beach-comber theme comes naturally to homes with the ocean more or less on the doorstep, like the California kitchen shown on these pages. Accessorize this driftwood style with natural textures – cotton, wicker and coir – in natural colours and the result will be a calm refuge from summer glare or city smog.

Wooden cupboards look most at home if you choose local woods – chestnut in France, oak in England, maple or cherry in America, pine in Scandinavia. For a genuine country feel cupboards should have solid, not veneered, fronts and be simple in construc-tion. Straightforward fielded panels or tongue-and-groove planking are more appropriate than the ornately fretted and panelled cabinets often sold as "country" styles by commercial kitchen companies.

The use of wood in a country kitchen does not have to be restricted to the furniture. You can introduce it in many ways – from the scrubbed and waxed planks of Shaker or Scandinavian floors to the grainy texture of American barn walls, the chunky open shelving of a French pantry or the mellow counters of an English kitchen.

COTTAGE
STYLE

The sort of country kitchens usually found in cottages, perhaps especially English cottage kitchens, are the most charming of all; cosy, crooked, cluttered, as jam-packed with things as a pedlar's tray. Valuable sits next to friendly tat, old next to new. The true cottage kitchen is so diminutive that when you open the back door the garden seems to spring into your lap.

A cottage kitchen can look unexpectedly dramatic treated to rich, contrasting colours. Here, green and crimson make an effective foil for the buttery glaze of brown and cream slipware. Red chillies and green herbs dangle in bunches from the ceiling, making a fortuitously colour-matched frieze.

Originally cottages did not have separate kitchens. Until the late 18th century, most ordinary country-dwelling families in Europe, along with the early settlers in America, lived, cooked and ate in the same room, cooking over an open fire on the hearth, usually in the black iron pot on a chain or tripod which figures in so many European folk tales.

The room that houses today's cottage kitchen is usually small because it has either been tacked onto the cottage at a later date or converted to its present use from a wash-house, animal byre or lean-to. Sometime in the 19th century a cast-iron range would would have been installed, and the earth floor paved over with practical, hard-wearing tiles.

In Scandinavia, cottage kitchens sometimes have cobbled floors; in Mediterranean countries smooth plaster or simple beaten earth was quite common.

The inspiration for today's idealized English-inspired version of the cottage kitchen is probably to be found in *The Tales of Beatrix Potter*, with their delectable watercolours of dressers crammed with painted china, geranium-packed windowsills framed by dimity curtains or drapes, and cosy fires fronted by polished brass fenders and multi-coloured rag rugs.

Small rooms can be tricky to plan, but they are fun to furnish and decorate. Cottage kitchen walls are often painted in warm, earthy terracotta, ochre or pink and brightened with stencils. They are then decorated with a patchwork of hanging shelves, little cupboards, plateracks, pictures, mementoes, even a straw hat wreathed in flowers. The

This Californian galley kitchen is a lesson in how to put bits and pieces together for the right effect. The owner's passion for all things floral has spread to the walls, with a magpie collection of flowery china, and tole trays hung on hooks that are easily anchored in the painted plank walls. A gutsy combed painted cupboard adds a note of toughness.

Cooking utensils are intrinsically decorative, so in a small cottage kitchen, where everything is on view, a row of ordinary ladles becomes a sculptural pelmet or valance above the window. Other elements are just as simple – from the classic pot sink raised on brick piers to the unusual cupboards either side of the sink. The pretty tile frieze has inspired a matching stencil border which meanders around doors, windows and ceiling.

kind of country kitchen where everything is on display is very suited to a small cottage setting as it allows for every inch of surface space – ceiling as well as wall – to be used for effective storage.

Exposed beams (luckily a frequent feature) carry baskets, bunches of herbs, strings of onions or dried sausages; lower down they bristle with cup hooks to take colanders, ladles, salt boxes.

Many cottage kitchens still harbour solid-fuel stoves, though the more up-to-date

manage to squeeze in a modern hob, cooktop or stove somewhere. Worktop or counter space is limited and the cottage kitchen's eating arrangements have to be flexible; perhaps a gateleg table that folds down when not in use, partnered by a Windsor wheel-back chair and a couple of stools.

Because cottage kitchens are often put together on a shoestring, they conform to the make-do and mend philosophy – nothing matches, but somehow the whole delightful mixture works.

All kinds of unusual antique materials – panelling, marble slabs rescued from fish-mongers' stores or old washstands, sturdy wooden butcher's blocks – can be salvaged and recycled.

One advantage of a small kitchen is that you have less area – floor, wall, worktop or counter – to cover. As a result, top-quality new materials like marble, hand-painted tiles or solid wood are more attainable, whatever your budget, because the yardage required is so little.

Stencils are quite at home in cottage kitch-ens, blending happily into this jumble of pattern and colour. They have a long history of cottage use: the humble folk of Europe, and later America, found them a simple and convenient tool with which to jolly up plain walls with traditional patterns.

Don't make the mistake of choosing fussy modern bows or roses; look for authentic folk designs like hearts, leaves or tulips. If you can't find an appropriate ready-made one, you could cut your own stencil. Trace off your chosen design, enlarging it with a photocopier if necessary, then transfer it to oiled stencil card and cut out the shapes with a sharp craft knife. Use a non-tack tape to fix the stencil in position on the wall. Then with an almost dry brush and an appropriate water-based paint, pounce on the colour through the cut card.

The rustic style of many cottage kitchens encourages the use of other traditional folksy paint finishes, such as combing and vinegar graining, on woodwork and cupboards.

Like much cottage furniture, these well-worn oak doors (above) have been recycled from a grander past. The tops (below) are of washstand marble, cut to fit.

FARMHOUSE
STYLE

Farmers were generally more prosperous than cottagers, and as a result the typical old farmhouse kitchen is a larger place altogether. You will find it solidly constructed, furnished with a substantial built-in dresser, a floor paved with stone, brick, slate or tiles and a hearth roomy enough to burn a Yule log if not roast an ox. Farmhouse kitchens also have a useful network of smaller store rooms, larders or pantries leading off them.

The kitchen of a working farm has too many calls upon it to look like anything you would see in a magazine. Muddy boots, wet dogs, steam from a hospitable kettle, drying clothes, stacks of agricultural journals and farm accounts in progress conspire against neatness and glossiness. But there is a warm, friendly atmosphere and the air is often sweet with baking.

Non-working farm kitchens are more likely to pander to the eye, though a certain ruggedness should properly remain. Matting and an easy chair or two are appropriate; frilly Austrian blinds or balloon shades are pushing it a bit. Use strong handsome colours for walls – Venetian red, ochre, olive green – as these make a fine setting for that fetish of the farm kitchen, the towering dresser blazing with colourful pottery and china. Vividly coloured, too, is that other important ingredient – the two-oven Aga in red, blue or green, glossy as a sports car. Once upon a time all farmhouse Agas had a clothes-drying rack on a pulley hooked up to the ceiling in front of them, but now most people favour a tumble drier.

In the larger farm kitchens there is a family room atmosphere, with cupboards and gadgets banked along one wall to leave more room for the odd comfy chair as well as that first essential of family life, a large, sturdy scrubbed table. To provide plenty of storage space you could entirely cover one wall with what appears to be an outsized dresser of the sort found in Victorian stately home kitchens. This should be commodious enough to

Such elegancies as wallpaper, matching fabric at the windows and leather-covered chairs are not out of place in a farmhouse kitchen, given a sympathetic treatment. As much dining area as kitchen, this room's utilitarian fittings have been played down by packing them along one wall and finishing them all in a pleasant honeyed pine. The focal point of the room, dramatized by ceiling spots, is a profusion of flowers and vegetable ornament – a frieze of herbs, wreaths of dried chillies, moss trees and a tablescape of potted cabbages.

cleverly incorporate larger pieces of equipment. It should include drawers, cubbyholes for wine bottles, shallow glazed cupboards for glasses and china, open shelves for displaying patterned china and storage jars and enough counter space to drop in a double sink.

This is decidedly a kitchen for eating in, and few people can resist advertising the fact by festooning their walls with wreaths or bunches of herbs, strings of onions, or that new accessory of the well-dressed kitchen, garlands of dark red chillies. Unless food habits have altered dramatically, these last must be for show rather than as the edible equivalent of gunpowder.

Farm kitchens may aspire to more formal occasions too, and where this happens a certain formality invades the furnishings – an ancestor's portrait on the wall, an iron chandelier above the table, a rug or two, even curtains. Space permitting, a curly-eaved French armoire is a wonderful extravagance to house the best china and glass, while the workday stuff lives on the dresser and the plate rack. Even kitchens with dishwashers have succumbed to plate racks because they are simply the most accessible, space-saving and attractive way to store plates that are in constant use.

It figures that the most distinctive farm kitchens must be found in the countries where rural culture remained intact and unthreatened for longest. Not merely countries, of course, but also regions. Tradition, doing things the way your forebears did them, shows up most forcefully in places off the beaten track, home to settled but small

communities of people mostly working and living off the land. Tuscany, Brittany, the West Coast of Ireland, the American Mid-West, Northumberland and Lincolnshire in England, are all places where you might expect to find things carrying on, and looking, much the way that they did a hundred years or so ago.

Scandinavia – Sweden, Denmark, Finland and Norway – retains more of its past, both in the form of old buildings and of old traditions and customs, than almost any area of comparable size. These northern countries remained largely peasant societies for longer than most; the industrial revolution reaching them seriously around the time that the 19th century gave way to the 20th. Visiting old farms, and cottages, in the Scandinavian countryside can give the most surprising sense of re-entering a past that still lives – orderly, frugal, intensely homey.

It hardly needs emphasizing that domestic life and the home have powerful importance in a climate which cuts people off, with deep snow and winter darkness, for a third to a half of the year. Scandinavians are fond of saying how home-loving they are, and this warm domesticity is clearly visible in the decoration of their old country houses.

Wood, softwood mainly, is the chief building material throughout northern Scandinavia, and their woodiness is the first thing that strikes you about most old Scandinavian buildings, inside and out. Many old farms began as peasant cottages, adding on rooms, storeys or separate wooden dwellings and outbuildings as the families prospered. Their modest beginnings are reflected in their unpretentious interiors, typically all wooden, of plank or log construction, with low ceilings, scrubbed bare floors, much built-in furniture and next to no casual clutter of possessions or superfluous furnishings.

Nowadays, Scandinavian homes are double- or triple-glazed and very efficiently heated, but many old farm kitchen-living rooms are still presided over by a *kakelung*, one of the towering ceramic stoves introduced during the 18th century, and an object of some envy to anyone who sees them. They come in many sizes and all styles, from flowery rococo to the gleaming simplicity, as of a ceramic column on a huge scale, of the neo-classical period. Nowadays these antique stoves are much sought after, with a brisk trade in restoring broken or incomplete examples.

Often, the parts are found hidden under the floorboards, where the workmen stowed them when they dismantled the stove half a century or so ago.

On the whole, Scandinavian farm kitchens are large and light, with many windows. But the older ones are often painted in quite dark, rich colours, with much use of painted marbling, spattered finishes, and a repertoire of patterns and effects created by a strong folk painting tradition. Against wooden walls painted green, gray or red-brown, vividly patterned doors on cupboards and dressers stand out as boldly as traditional wool embroideries do on the regional costumes worn on festive days. An extra-special piece of freestanding furniture – a marriage chest or a longcase clock – may be brightly decorated over every inch of its surface. These are heirlooms now, and much prized.

However, despite the prevalence of painted colour, which makes these old farmhouse kitchens so different from the cool, almost clinical interiors associated with modern Scandinavian design, the dominant impression is of the warmth, dignity and friendliness of all-wood rooms, in which so much else, including the furniture, the utensils and the

A traditional farmhouse kitchen, complete with beams, quarry tiles and a generous brick hearth, is enlivened by a bold use of colour. Walls and ceilings are painted a glowing red, a rich foil for the collection of antique furniture and artefacts. And a clever mix of deep blue and red give a run of built-in cupboards a military smartness. The red-sponged walls are lightened with a lacy white border, which on closer inspection turns out to be a farmhouse, repeated like a motif embroidered on a sampler.

containers, is wooden too.

Wood is unquestionably the most humane material to live with in cold climates. It is hardly surprising that the Scandinavian emigrants to the New World took their wood technology with them. Thus Americans

A traditional raised hearth, whitewashed like the rest of this Swedish kitchen, provides a comforting blaze to eat beside as well as creating a natural break between the working and dining areas.

inherited the art of constructing log cabins and of fixing up weatherboard or plank walls, plus the tradition of building in a good deal of kitchen furniture, sturdily, of massively thick pine and fir.

The good looks of wooden walls in kitchens,

and their readiness to take anything from tiers of shelves to rows of pans or decorative bygones, is immediately clear from looking at so many Scandinavian and American farmhouse-style kitchens in this book. They inspire anyone who has inherited a kitchen

Well-worn chairs are found in farmhouse kitchens the world over. These are characteristic of 18th-century Swedish furniture, the result of subjecting linseed oil and white lead paint to generations of use.

that was clad in planking during the stripped pine phase of the 1960s or 1970s. Newly painted, rather than varnished (which made them orange as well as shiny), their walls have a serviceableness which should bring them right back into fashion.

Below: Strong blocks of iron-oxide red set off against whitewashed walls and ceiling make an abstract painting of this austere but handsome Colonial kitchen. All details of the original room have been faithfully retained, right down to the small bread oven set in the brick wall to the left of the hearth and an iron kettle suspended over a wood fire.

Right: Against the calm simplicity of this kitchen, the colours of the vegetables piled on the table sing out.

Left: The owner's honest approach to decorating a country home is evident in the small mud room that adjoins the kitchen, with its plank walls and door and Shaker pegs for hats and coats.

MANOR-HOUSE
STYLE

A certain grandeur, or dignity at least, attaches to the lofty and spacious kitchens where meals for the gentry were once prepared and cooked by anything from half a dozen kitchen staff upward. As a rule, servants did not eat in the kitchen in manor houses of any pretension, but in a servants' hall. Stately homes, like Lord Lichfield's Shugborough, have kitchens like cathedrals, long-windowed, with tables 20 feet (6 metres) long, tier-upon-tier of shelving displaying an armoury of scoured copper pans and utensils and a whole congeries of utilitarian side-chapels, the game room, still-room, pantry, dairy and so forth.

Attempting to cosy up and live in rooms of this scale is out of the question, but luckily most manor or manorial-scale houses in Europe or America are relatively modest in size and their kitchens lend themselves to a family take-over. These are rooms where planning and installing a roomful of cupboards seems pointless; there is so much space to spare that the wisest course is to keep the place warm and allow various family activities to pile in. Thus there may well be a cooking part, an eating area and a corner furnished with a comfortable sofa for relaxing. In more eccentric kitchens of this type, in Ireland for instance, there may be a snooker table, or a piano, too.

One manorial feature that enviably remains, as a rule, is a big open fire that acts as a necessary supplement to a four-oven Aga. Some good furniture will have crept in from the rest of the house, marking the upgrading of the room. These touches of grandeur may include family portraits, gilt mirrors, or a

Above and below: What raises the manor-house style a notch above the farmhouse is the scale of the space. This encourages a certain formality in the design – ancestral portraits, candelabra and polished oak look quite in keeping. The country feel is retained with rustic accessories.

Right: Manor-house kitchens are roomy enough to take a sofa and chairs, as well as dining furniture.

marble-topped buffet that acts as sideboard. These large, if sparsely detailed, rooms are naturally home to large, swaggering items of furniture. Typical pieces include immense breakfront bookcases, which store preserves and china as well as cookbooks; six-fold screens that break up the vast spaces and cut out the drafts that are so common in large old houses; and entire painted Scandinavian cupboard beds, now doubling as seating. In such a large room you should also have space for a dresser or two; stand spare dining chairs either side and hang a picture – a portrait of a venerable ancestor or an ancestor's horse – above to fill up wall space. Such gestures suit the scale and this sort of furniture provides ample storage for a wealth of inherited possessions.

Kitchens are, of course, a suitable venue for any decorative art with food connotations, and the manor-house kitchen has enough space for these to be of a large, dramatic nature. I know a kitchen in East Anglia dominated by a life-size, gilded and carved wooden pig, a fortunate spin-off from the demolition of an old butcher's shop. In the same spirit are the cut-out painted figures of both people and animals known as "silent companions". A kitchen I visited in Normandy has a pair of these, a milkmaid and a soldier boy, standing either side of a massive brick hearth.

The most suitable flooring for a kitchen in this style is probably one that continues over both living and working areas – probably hand-made tiles, bricks or flagstones. You can then soften the living areas with kelims or rugs to help the furnished look along.

This impressive kitchen has space
enough to take a splendid antique
armoire and table, as well as a four-
oven Aga. A brass rail hangs cooking
implements within easy reach, while
no less than two ceiling-hung racks
take care of all the pots, pans, sieves
and colanders. A marble-topped table
(above) houses bowls and platters
conveniently to hand. An adjoining
alcove (below) is fitted out in the style
of a china closet.

A stretch of colourful antique ceramic tiles, natural wood cupboards, a useful shelf above the window for platters and jugs, warm terracotta tiles on the floor all add up to a kitchen that seems exuberantly Spanish and Mediterranean at the same time. Designer Jaime Parlade mixes antique with contemporary, decorative with functional and local with foreign with assured ease.

NATIONAL
—STYLES—

For the most part, the styles of country kitchen that find favour all over the world today originate in a strong tradition of building in local materials to suit a rural way of life that has never died. Unassuming, honest, these kitchens have a natural integrity that many modern kitchens lack. Often, for the same reasons, the country food of the area has also had an influence far beyond the borders of the district. Provence in France and Tuscany in Italy are prime examples of this.

This section of the book provides a visual gazetteer to the foremost national styles – from England, France, Italy, Spain and America – that have travelled beyond their own boundaries. Each style provides a wealth of design ideas that you can copy or adapt for your country kitchen, wherever you may live.

AMERICAN
KITCHENS

The earliest American kitchens often surprise by their spaciousness. They are closer in type to the wealthy English landowner's hall, with their beamed ceilings, great open hearths and tough flooring of brick or stone flags, than they are to the cramped, dark quarters where most of the pioneers' impoverished European forefathers contrived to prepare, cook and eat their daily meals. Perhaps the sheer scale of the newly settled lands was an invitation to think bigger. On the whole, however, American colonial buildings and interiors were modelled on the homes in which the colonists – British, German, Dutch, French and Scandinavian – had grown up in back in Europe. Like expatriates everywhere, they clung onto their native traditions, partly because they were familiar, tried and tested, and partly because the old ways gave a sense of continuity that made the colonists strong enough to survive uprooting and starting over in a New World. The English favoured panelling and sturdy oak furniture, while the Germans

and Dutch liked brightly decorated furniture and plank walls painted, or later stencilled, with simple homemade colours based on cheaply available ingredients like earth, buttermilk or linseed oil.

In the earliest American kitchens paint was used as a protective finish for pine or softwood panelling or furniture. Paint colours were traditional – sober and deep but rich in hue – and in the more austere Puritan-influenced interiors at least, would have been applied quite plainly, without further decoration. As more and more immigrants entered America from countries belonging to the so-called "conifer culture" (from Russia via Eastern Europe to Germany and Scandinavia), American country kitchens began to bloom with the strong colours and vivid traditional painted motifs that were a frequent element in the homes of 19th century European peasants.

New arrivals either brought their furniture with them or copied their traditional designs in native American woods. Such pieces

included chests, armoires, display cabinets with doors hinged to stand open, hanging shelves and small cupboards, dressers of every shape and size and benches with swivel backs, as well as a mass of colourfully decorated small items such as birch bark boxes, ladles and spoons. Whatever the context – log cabin or stone-built farmhouse – pieces like these brought inside heart-warming colour and pattern, as welcome in the New World as it had been in the Old.

Decoratively painted pieces were status symbols in their day, telling the world that this was a family which had progressed further than the mere struggle for survival. As in Europe, American pieces were usually painted and decorated by professionals, often itinerant, who moved in for a few days, or weeks, and left behind them a gorgeous trail of colour and pattern – hearts, birds and flowers, painted freehand or stencilled, sweeps of bold marbling or wild and non-realistic graining, as well as a copious scattering of inscriptions, mottoes and initials.

Rugged woody textures stamp this kitchen as early American in style. In fact, the building is an old barn, reworked to make a country house. The owners have kept colour to a minimum – a few painted chairs and a wall cupboard – so that the wood has as much impact as possible. The frontier mood is enhanced by oil lamps hooked to the beams at strategic points – an interesting alternative to candelabra for period-style lighting.

The new country was rich in timber, so woodiness is a characteristic of many snug and solid old-fashioned American kitchens. They often have a rugged dignity, a sparseness and an absence of superfluities which seem newly American – at once an inheritance of a Puritan outlook and a reflection of the priorities of pioneer life, where anything needed had to be built, whittled, painted, stitched or otherwise improvized.

The old kitchen-cum-living rooms were known as "keeping rooms" and were often, as in European peasant homes, where people slept and worked as well as cooked. They are the prototype of what today is marketed as an unstructured or "unfitted" kitchen. Once created out of necessity, this look is re-created deliberately today for comfort and friendliness. The ingredients are few and need not be expensive if you put them together yourself instead of relying on the custom-made unstructured or "unfitted" collections available. Finding the ingredients will be fun,

if time-consuming. If you are short of time rather than cash, you should plump for a well-crafted and intelligently thought-out designer set.

It would be difficult to imagine anything further removed from a streamlined, built-in contemporary kitchen than the early American type, where almost everything in daily use – amounting to a fraction of what we would think necessary – is out in the open, suspended from hooks or ranged along shelves. Kitchen equipment really worked for its living in the days when imported wares were scarce and expensive, shops and stores few and far between and leisure time non-existent. There is a rare comeliness about many of the simple objects that our ancestors used continually – the wooden flour bins, iron cooking pots and trivets, hand-carved wooden spoons, salt-glazed brown jars and pots, scribbly patterned slipware and cloudy old glass.

To recreate the atmosphere of an early

American interior go for an unstructured look and rugged, natural materials. Sheath the walls and ceiling of a new room with tongue-and-groove panelling to give a more sympathetic feel and make a handsome background for painted furniture and other period items. Fit a decorative wooden cornice to neaten the effect.

All the wood should be painted rather than left bare, using one of the subtle colours of the period – barn red, blueberry or Williamsburg green. Many American paint firms have a "country colour" range (see page 176). And some specialist firms produce old-style paints like buttermilk paint or limewash, which give the matte, "lean" texture of aged paintwork. Wooden walls are great for kitchens because they make the task of hanging up shelves and so forth supremely easy. Any new or built-in pieces you cannot do without can be blended in very simply by painting them in the same colour as the tongue-and-groove walls.

Left: The colour scheme of this handsome Colonial style kitchen – rusty-red ochre paint and tawny natural wood with buttermilk-coloured plank walls – is reproduced aloft in a still life of nubbly baskets, strings of dried corncobs and garlands of red chillies. Wooden walls make the ideal pegboard for old iron cornbread moulds, while to the right of an unobtrusive modern stove an improvized chandelier of kitchen hooks spikes a charming collection of little baskets. This small space feels purposefully crowded rather than cluttered; details like the pottery jars packed with well-worn implements are evidence that this kitchen is for use rather than display.

Left: The comeliness of natural things decorates this kitchen: old mixing bowls heaped with apples, garlic heads, bundled herbs. Good cooks work like this, surrounding themselves with the tools and materials of their craft as inspiration.

Against this background of sober but warm and unified colour, introduce gaiety and contrast with decoratively painted furniture in the Pennsylvania Dutch style, a collection of bright pottery, hooked or rag rugs, or a combination of all three. Today, genuine old country pieces are hard to find, and expensive to buy, but there are excellent reproductions available that can be improved with brightly stencilled motifs or a tawny-coloured, vinegar-grained finish.

The American-style country kitchen should be furnished with a solid, generously sized table that is nearer to a refectory shape (a long rectangle) than the standard offering. Such tables, usually of pine and scrubbed to a bleached pallor by daily applications of cleanser and elbow grease, turn up all the time in country-style antique shops; oak tables of the right period and sturdy simplicity turn up less often. Used for preparing food as much as for serving and eating it, this table needs to be surrounded by equally simple but relaxed-looking chairs. These

A Connecticut home bursting with appealingly dilapidated old cupboards – the more scuffed, the better – shows how these give warmth and atmosphere to what is otherwise a fairly conventional kitchen with a full complement of modern appliances. The dining area shows more of the owner's collection of old North American pieces. Her skill lies in grouping colours – a green platter, mustard table, misty blue doors.

could be a harlequin or unmatched set collected at auctions and junk shops. Basic checked squabs or cushions can be added for comfort, but these chairs, like everything else in the old-style kitchen, should not look fussy or formal.

An unstructured American kitchen should also have a splendid breadth of shelving. Either install a genuine old dresser or commission a carpenter to run off a stack of shelves, maybe with one or two cut-out flourishes, to fit over a bank of kitchen cupboards. Use these shelves to accommodate china in daily use – teapots, jugs, cups and mugs on hooks – and that sea-wrack of family flotsam and jetsam which tidy-minded people are always struggling to organize or eliminate.

Cast-iron ranges, whether antique or new, are the most appropriate form of stove, giving off splendid warmth as well as providing the ideal even heat for baking and simmering. Antique solid fuel stoves can often be converted to gas or oil-fired systems.

If the original fireplace exists you should retain it as firelight will add a special touch to any evening meal.

Perhaps the two items which most underline an early American feel are a rocking chair and an iron or tin chandelier to hang above the long scrubbed table. Hooking your own rug or making a patchwork pillow cover for the rocker is just the kind of traditional winter evening occupation which will help give your American country kitchen the authentic folksy flavour.

Shaker Style

19th century America's largest and best-known communal religious society, the Shakers, lived by the daily philosophy "hands to work and hearts to God". Order, cleanliness and industry were articles of Shaker faith. Shakers believed that things should first of all be useful, but that usefulness did not preclude perfection in the design and making of a piece. Today, the Shaker community is virtually non-existent, but their designs have a very wide influence.

The Shakers have become famous for the perfect workmanship which goes into everything their communities produce, but above all for their simple, finely crafted furniture made from native American woods like pine, maple, butternut or cherry. Shakers frowned upon superfluities of any kind in the design and making of such things, so Shaker cupboard handles are smooth, plain round knobs, neat as buttons, while their chair seats are of simple but strong coloured webbing. The aesthetic purity of Shaker style has obvious affinities with contemporary minimalism and its refinement and practicality suits a busy late 20th century lifestyle.

There is a mistaken belief that Shakers forbade the use of colour. But although most Shaker interiors were smoothly plastered and painted plain white, interior woodwork was often finished in a blue, gray, black or dark green matte paint. And some Shaker boxes and pieces of furniture were stained or painted in strong, deep colours. However, paint was always quite plainly applied; the use of fancy paint finishes, while undoubtedly decorative, goes against the spirit of Shaker design.

Avoid non-essentials, hunt out fine workmanship, keep everything fastidiously clean and tidy and a Shaker kitchen will provide a serene and calming space as well as an efficient, orderly cooking environment.

Happily, built-in cupboards are authentic to Shaker style – they used them wherever possible, for orderliness. One innovation of Shaker design that is particularly useful in a kitchen context is the peg rail running around the walls. Its simple polished wooden pegs inserted at regular intervals serve to display kitchen tools, baskets or hanging shelves.

Shaker chairs are in the rustic tradition, with straight legs, woven seats and ladder-backs. Shakers preferred uniformity, so chairs should match. Save up and buy them two at a time, to partner the plainest pine drop-leaf or refectory-style table.

Accessories and equipment should be of the simplest traditional shapes and materials – plain white china to eat off and beautifully woven baskets to hold fresh produce. Treat yourself to one or two oval boxes, with their distinctive swallowtail joints secured with copper rivets, to hold special things. Build up a small collection of old implements such as ladles, colanders, sieves and flat brooms to hang from your peg rail and break up the bareness of the white walls.

FRENCH
—KITCHENS—

Until recently, the French have paid considerably more attention to what comes out of a kitchen in the way of food than to what goes into it in the way of furniture and equipment. A French kitchen was primarily functional, a workplace, and most French families ate their meals in the dining room. Changing lifestyles and a new emphasis on home design have had their effect on modern French kitchens. Today they contain many more gadgets than they once did. In addition, they are newly preoccupied with planning, comfort and good looks now that they often double as a venue for family meals.

But traditional elements linger on, even so, and it is often these that impart a distinctively French flavour and charm. How many

There is something instantly recognizable as French in this kitchen from the Ile de Re. The French flair for improvization is evident in details like the dishtowel lampshade or the crisp white matelasse bedspread used to make a handsome tablecloth. An idea worth copying is the glazed 2-way serving hatch, fitted between working kitchen and dining area and used to house glasses. Crochet edging to the shelves plus the sparkle of the backlit glasses themselves make this functional feature decorative too. Another clever stroke of French savoir faire is the series of knife slots very simply cut into one end of a shelf.

British or American cooks would continue edging their shelves with decorative cut-paper borders, still less with the bands of cotton crochet shown here. Note how the glazed storage cupboard for glasses serves rooms on either side; this is an attractive solution to the problem of what to do with a serving hatch that has become redundant in a home where the family eats in their kitchen. On the practical side, what could be simpler and more devastatingly logical than cutting slots in a wooden shelf, worktop or counter for storing knives out of harm's way but within easy reach of the busy cook? Of course, you must ensure that the blades are safely housed beneath.

For most people, buying the traditional cast-

Ingenious ideas from a converted inn in Provence: a collection of old-fashioned slates, one for every day of the week, is used for messages, shopping lists or reminders, while the built-in bottle rack is made up of hexagonal breeze blocks, simply colourwashed.

Right: Narrow doors are of limed chestnut, in an unusual chevron arrangement. The far wall appears to be of bricks, but is in fact all trompe l'oeil – the bricks are painted in shades of pink and terracotta onto plain plaster. The acid yellow and rich green pottery set out on the dinner table is unmistakably of Provençal provenance.

iron cookware by such firms as Le Creuset is the easiest way to introduce a French note to the kitchen. These pots and pans remain unsurpassed for slow simmering and braising, and their good looks take them to the table without apology.

French pottery, too, has found its way into kitchens all over the world. Whatever your taste, some dish, platter or bowl is probably already installed in your home, whether it be the chunky Provençal ware decorated in rich green or ochre glazes or the prettier flower-strewn products from French potteries like Quimper.

Many antique dealers in both Europe and America stock the appealing 19th century French shop and café furniture such as display stands of curly metal and marble, or glass, which once held tempting selections of patisseries or charcuterie. Today, these can be used as decorative serving tables in kitchens where space is not at a premium.

Other French antiques that add flavour to a medium- or large-sized kitchen include capacious armoires or buffets for storing china and linen, and the wonderfully curly wood-burning stoves used for heating.

Of course, the final touch for any French-style kitchen is the food – dishes like the rabbit terrine on page 139 or the chocolate cake on page 164 will bring an instant flavour of France into your home.

This French-style kitchen has been slotted into the garden-level floor of a late 18th century London house. The flagged floor, huge range and pretty iron chandelier contribute to the French atmosphere, as do the gingham-checked walls and natural wood cupboards and shelves. The woodwork is lightly "grained" to match the colour of the antique armoire. Lined in sprigged French cotton, the armoire plays host to a collection of brightly glazed Provençal pottery mixed with daintier white porcelain. It is flanked by an elegant cast-iron pot stand. The glazed top panels to the connecting doors allow sunlight to flood into the room.

SPANISH
—KITCHENS—

Azulejo is the Spanish word for the vivid ceramic tiles which have been produced in Andalusia for over a thousand years, since the region was ruled over by the Moors. You can see their Islamic ancestors lining the walls of the Alhambra, summer palace of the Moorish kings.

Set off by whitewashed walls, the warm, uneven tones of terracotta floor tiles and a bank of handsomely crafted cabinets in pale native wood, the generous use of richly patterned ceramic tiles will give any kitchen a distinctively Spanish flavour. Antique versions, like those shown here, are much sought after and expensive in Spain today, but can occasionally be found more cheaply elsewhere in Europe, as can modern reproductions. For example, Portugal exports a great deal of colourful, inexpensive ceramic tiles, as well as crockery and other kitchen accessories, which have the right sort of look. Hand-made terracotta floor tiles now come in a wide variety of shapes and sizes. Their varying tones and slightly irregular shapes are part of their appeal, and they look best laid with a wide grouting line – about an inch or 2 centimetres all around.

Trawling through street markets on trips to Spain or Portugal should yield a cache of glazed storage jars, oven dishes and crockery in simple, traditional shapes and glorious colours – vivid green, sharp lemon-yellow, chestnut-brown.

Working with plaster in a free-form, sculptural style is an old skill of Mediterranean peoples. Although born of poverty and shortage of materials, this form of plasterwork has great natural dignity when executed by

Right: Vivid old tiles in shades of blue on white make a beguiling but practical wall-covering in this Spanish kitchen. Old ceramic jars and pots for coffee and eggs are in the same spirit, folksy but handsome. Decoratively cut-out boards bristling with iron hooks act like a peg board, receiving a wonderful assortment of kitchen paraphernalia. The knife rack and sink are unaffectedly modern.

Below: Painting the inside of a pine dresser in a soft blue highlights colourful china.

a master tradesman and kept brightly white by regular limewashing. Plaster and render over concrete, stone, or (these days) breezeblocks, allows considerable freedom in designing and shaping all the elements of a kitchen, from a hooded alcove to take the cooker or range, to open-fronted storage cubbyholes below worktops or counters. Expert workmanship gives a seamless, streamlined quality – nicely rounded angles where other forms of construction invariably create awkward cracks, joints and dust-collecting crevices.

Until quite recently this type of plasterwork was a standard feature of country kitchens in Spain, particularly in the South. It was standard in the poorer dwelling, the peasant or fisherman's cottage, but it was also to be found in the large but austerely appointed kitchens of many more pretentious villas.

I remember becoming adept at cooking on a primitive range fired by wood and charcoal in a villa near Alicante; the villa had a great tangled garden full of lemon trees and vines, and a stunning view over a small rocky cove, but the kitchen was as basic as can be, dark, viewless and sparsely furnished. The explanation, of course, is that the family who lived in the villa had servants, a cook and maids, inured to working in difficult conditions, or rather conditions that strike us now as bleak or difficult, but are a little better than those that met the domestic servants in an 18th century London terrace house. There, the cook and kitchenmaid frequently slept in the basement kitchen, on pallets rolled up and put away by day.

The cubbyhole form of storage that is

moulded from plaster, but with shelves of thick wood and, often, with an inset tiled worktop or counter is convenient as well as attractive, provided that it can be kept spotless, free of mice and cockroaches. These storage systems are custom built to fit the space available. Cubbyholes feel like the natural place to stow the large, heavy earthenware dishes and bowls so commonly used in Spanish cookery. However, they should not be too deep from front to back, because crouching down to reach far into a space is tedious and bad for the back.

Although most large pieces of equipment are stored away in the cubbyholes, some items, like the *paellera*, or huge round iron pan used to make that celebrated fishy rice dish, usually hang off the wall.

Floors in old Spanish kitchens were not uncommonly plastered too, often with colour mixed into the plaster which was then polished with steel floats. These floors would be rounded off where they meet the walls.

Cupboards were easily contrived by fitting shelves across a plastered alcove and hanging doors off the front. Spanish doors would

Above: This "rustic" Spanish kitchen carries poignant reminders of Mediterranean holidays in rented cottages and villas. Full of charm, it is probably as practical to cook in as a much more streamlined place. An unplaned plank makes a robust edge to the little working corner, topped by a basic two-ring hob or cooktop, while curtained shelves beneath are one of those inexpensive makeshifts that really work, and suit their unpretentious setting.

Above: The kitchen abuts the living area, but is separated from it by a typically Spanish plaster structure at floor level. Under the counter huge terracotta pots veiled with gauze and capped with local cork contain a Spanish country cook's handiwork: home-made goat's cheeses marinating in olive oil.

Above right: A collection of baskets on a marble-topped table is all the pantry this kitchen needs.

be solid and handsomely detailed. The decorative wooden lattice door panel that is found throughout Portugal, Spain and the Greek islands seems to be an import to the Mediterranean area from North Africa. It was most likely designed to keep the cupboard's contents airy and cool. Simple as they look, the lattices are of quite elaborate construction, much more complex than mere trellis.

Modern Spanish kitchens, as our examples show, have made a positive move toward lightness and brightness, a celebration of an enviably sunny climate. Plasterwork still features, but now partnered by excellent joinery and gorgeous ceramics, old and new. The judicious add a few rush-seated chairs, stained deep blue or red, a table under an umbrella or vine-draped loggia outside in the courtyard or verandah, lots of inexpensive, bright crockery, bowls brimming with fruit and glass jugs full of sangria.

In fact, the Spanish kitchen will often extend onto the verandah or terrace outside, where food will be grilled over charcoal or wood on a plaster or brick-built barbecue.

ITALIAN
—KITCHENS—

An inspired use of colour seems bred into the Italian make-up, an instinct so ancient and easy that the Italians themselves take it for granted. The colours that come to mind first are those of Italian cities, villages and ports – the warm earth pigments, with their Italian names, burnt sienna, raw sienna, burnt and raw umber, ochres red and yellow and Venetian red. Italy was, after all, the cradle of fine art.

But there is another earthy product associated with Italy, and perhaps kitchens especially. This product is earthenware, or fired clay, in all its guises from the humblest bean pot with a glazed lining to the joyful gaudiness of maiolica and the crude, but vivid spongeware of Sicily and southern Italy.

Italian kitchens, especially in the country, are often primitive, but they have a special glow of colour and a warm ease of texture, compounded of flaky, colourwashed plaster, a generous use of tiling (in jewel as well as earth tones) and a certain friendly copiousness in their *batterie de cuisine* which has much

to do with a tradition of making the staple foods – pasta, rice, polenta – stretch hospitably further by eking them out with home-made cheeses and freshly picked herbs, tomatoes and fungi, and washing them down with unpretentious home-made wines. The world at large thinks of Italy and pasta in the same breath, but other staple foods, like rice, beans and polenta are equally Italian, although more regional in character. These dishes were often cooked in special pots, like the tapering earthenware bean pot which could be left simmering slowly for several hours without any danger of too much surface evaporation that would result in the bean pottage drying out. Polenta was traditionally cooked in a heavy iron or copper pot with a rounded base, to prevent the maize mixture catching and burning. It was served up on a large, scrubbed wooden board, looking in the words of the Italian writer, Alessandro Manzoni, "like a harvest moon in a large circle of mist". The perfect risotto is cooked in a heavy copper or

enamelled cast-iron pan, preferably with a rounded base. It must be large enough for the rice to expand to almost three times its dry volume.

There is a genial quality about Italian country cooking, at once simple and sensuous. Food may be basic, but great care and style is involved in gathering and cooking the ingredients. Old women still spend hours searching the fields and lanes for wild leaves or herbs and fungi to flavour risottos and pastas. This attitude communicates itself not only to the equipment and containers used to prepare and present it – generously scaled bowls, boards and platters – but also to the kitchens in which it is produced.

Italian country kitchens are a world away from their sleekly sophisticated city cousins. Their walls are often cracked and peeling, their paint fading, their gadgets conspicuous by their absence. However, there is usually a touch of grandeur mixed in with the effects of time and wear. A copious use of local marble, for instance, is often combined with wooden

Left: Italian country kitchen furniture often includes stylish improvization like this simple linen chest laden with cookbooks, flowering herbs and bowls of apples.

Right: Dining space in Italian kitchens is usually restricted to a small sliver of a table for hasty breakfasts (far right). Informal meals are often eaten outdoors; more formal feasts in a separate dining room.

Left: An island sited opposite the stoves (two side by side) provides an easily accessible counter as well as a rallying point for informal, pasta-based family meals. A curly wrought-iron rack, traditionally Tuscan, holds a selection of pans.

Below: Memories of Tuscany inspired the rich burnt sienna colouring of the walls and ceiling in this Californian country home. Terracotta floor tiles link the dining space to the adjoining tightly organized Italian-style kitchen (shown left).

cabinet doors and rustic kitchen equipment that is handsomely carved. The plasterwork may be a little flaky, but it is usually tinted a gentle and distinguished colour, reminiscent of fresco work. There is much terracotta, glazed and unglazed, soberly undecorated for cooking with, but extravagantly colourful in the maiolica tradition for tableware.

In her evocative book *Honey from a Weed* (see p.180), essential reading for all devotees of the kitchen, one of my favourite cookery writers, Patience Gray, describes a kitchen she visited at Luni. Belonging to the guardian of the Temple of Diana, this reads like a characteristically Italian mixture of the pri-

mitive and the fastidious. It has a red brick floor, a high ceiling of whitewashed beams, a big hearth, a bottle-gas stove, a table, chairs and a settle.

She continues: "Behind the settle was an array of copper and aluminium pans suspended from a wooden framework on the wall. At the window was a stone sink, the drinking water kept in a large terracotta Tuscan bowl with a glaze of green marbling inside. The cheese was kept in the kitchen drawer out of the way of the cats and the bread in the bread chest. The *cantina* across the passage was well-stocked with wine, both white and red".

ENGLISH
—KITCHENS—

Any lingering doubts about the English interest in food must surely be dispelled by the well-used, much-loved air of the kitchens shown on these pages. The people who chose these colours, put together these pieces of furniture, collected and arranged dresser displays of such glorious diversity, are serious about cooking and eating. They also care a great deal about creating a good atmosphere around these two essential activities.

It is easy to see why British influence on interior design has become so important over the last decade or so; the English kitchens are visually innovative, romantically individual and rampantly eclectic. There is the odd austere, traditional kitchen – stone, slate, whitewash and scrubbed deal – but more typical of today is somewhere cosy, cluttered, colourful, creating an effect halfway between a donnish study and an artist's studio.

Cottage kitchens squeezed into their low-ceilinged, much-beamed back extensions are perhaps the most quintessentially English in spirit – quaint, nooky, inconvenient (to a purist designer), but as informally appealing as a traditional cottage garden.

The possessors of these charming kitchens have never consulted tomes on kitchen planning and ergonomics; more likely, they were inspired by the romantic watercolour illustrations of wooden dressers packed with china or blackleaded stoves finished with twinkling brasswork that are found in *The Tales of Beatrix Potter*.

The British today, it is abundantly clear, gain enormous fun out of making kitchens in their own image, kitchens that are not designed to impress, but created to please and give enjoyment.

Nostalgia is very evident in the magpie nest effect of so many things lovingly distributed over walls, ceilings, every available surface. It is almost as if there is a powerful urge to squirrel away some bits and pieces of the national past before it is all shipped away to Tokyo, Los Angeles or Milan.

One respect in which English kitchens differ from others is in their penchant for mixing the strictly culinary with items like books and pictures that no Italian or Spanish cook would admit to their workplace. Shelves of books, mostly, but not all, cookery and wine titles, undoubtedly give any kitchen a civilized, Bloomsburyish atmosphere which the English have always found sympathetic.

The English are great collectors of unconsidered trifles – old printed tins, odd eggcups or china – and even the tiniest English kitchen is a natural home for these. Fashionable ideas do infiltrate – rustic chandeliers one year, stencils another, but they never dominate. There is a self-assurance about English country kitchens, a confident handling of effects that makes them among the most fascinating of all – though perhaps not to the English.

Right: You could hardly get further from stainless steel sinks and waste disposals, but for all its apparent random clutter and lack of mod cons this little washing-up corner has everything conveniently to hand – shelves, racks, a cubbyhole for cleaning materials.

Right: In this period-style English kitchen a little alcove beside the dining table holds useful items for the table, while nicely worn and weathered wooden bread and cheese boards pick up the rugged texture of the old butcher's block above. Cleared of decorative bits and pieces, the block makes a splendid chopping area.

Things have so invaded every inch of this English cottage kitchen that decoration takes second place to a patchwork of possessions, colourful in themselves. A handsome set of polished Windsor chairs provide substantial seating around a table covered with patterned cotton, yellow for cheer, plasticized for convenience. A collection of potbellied casseroles and jars is a reminder that country pottery is often too good-looking to be put away out of sight.

A magnificent floor of riven Cornish slate (underfloor heated) is the handsomest feature of a cool, dairy-like kitchen in Cornwall, where the only splash of colour comes from a row of splendidly decorative plates that make a frieze above a small window dressed in blue and white gingham. Work counters on the simple white-painted tongue-and-groove cupboards are of slate to match the floor. Strap hinges have been painted white to match and doorhandles are white china. Note the dog bed in the corner, home to the Englishman's best friend.

Limited space has been put to intelligent use to incorporate all the country standards in this efficient but friendly-looking kitchen. Open shelves to the right of the sink hold a whole battery of pots and pans, while cooking implements dangle from a wall-mounted rack to the right of the Aga recess. A butler's sink with teak drainers is set off by the smooth dark green paint on all the cupboards.

— KITCHEN —
DETAILS

Detailing, in the architectural sense of requirements met and problems solved, gives any kitchen an orderly framework which lightens a cook's work. When carried through to fastidious standards of design and craftsmanship, as in the country kitchens shown on these pages, details – whether they are well-restored original features or newly installed elements – are also a major source of aesthetic pleasure.

What there is should be of the best quality, from wood-block, stone-flagged or terracotta-tiled floor, to an heirloom range set in its tiled alcove to an old-fashioned ceramic butler's sink dropped into a beautifully crafted frame of scrubbed teak or marble. Such traditional details will add an appropriately timeless mood to the newest of country kitchens.

SURFACES

Traditional wisdom has always seen to it that kitchen surfaces destined for hard use – worktops or counters, sink surrounds, floor, hearth – should be made of the best materials available locally. Best here meant durable and cleanly rather than beautiful, but one result of living in the age of plastics is that we look at the sturdy traditional materials like slate, wood and glazed earthenware with newly appreciative eyes. We see them as both handsome and genuine, adding their own integrity to kitchen life and activity.

If you are trying to recreate a particular national style in your kitchen you should always choose genuine regional materials for all the surfaces. For example, brightly patterned tiles (see p.61) and free-form plaster structures (see p.63) will give your kitchen an

Right: In Cornwall, which provided the kitchen, the fish and the slate, several colours of indigenous slate are available – not just mackerel blue-black, but soft greens and grays too. Slate is not warm-looking, like wood, but it is hygienic. Scour it daily, then bring up its cool sheen by wiping with milk or a light oil.

Below: The first requirement of kitchen surfaces is that they should be sturdy enough to take a lot of wear and tear, but at the same time sympathetic and friendly. Old-fashioned terracotta fits these requirements perfectly, with its warm tones and earthy textures.

authentic Spanish flavour, while rugged wood (see pp.46-7) epitomizes the American country kitchen.

Contemporary kitchen designers have adopted that practical idea that has always been a feature of country kitchens – work surfaces or counters of different depths, set at different heights.

The traditional kitchen surface materials all have their own attributes, and current thinking in kitchen design is that people should put together an eclectic selection of surfaces that suits their personal needs and tastes. For instance, slate, stone and marble are matchless for toughness, and their natural chilliness makes them ideal for rolling out pastry and pasta, or as larder shelving, but too much of any of these makes a kitchen feel

A quirky imagination was at work assembling the surfaces of this Californian kitchen, where cool, watery overall tones suddenly crackle with the hot colours of a Mexican huarache or handwoven throw. Granite counters are routine these days, but the twist here is that the perimeter is left rough and wavy, as if just hewn from the rock. And the *pique-assiette tiling on the wall makes a splashback with 'craquelure' appeal, nicely offset by dry brush work in blue-green on the painted cupboards.*

clammy, like a cellar. They magnify noise too, and not just the smash of breaking crockery and glasses.

Slate is a superbly handsome natural material which develops intense colour when wet, but dries to a dusty hue unless wiped over from time to time with oil or milk. Close-grained and cool, it was traditionally used for dairy shelves. Latterly, granite, which used to be relegated to bank lobbies and monumental masonry, is the most popular of the hard-surfacing materials. It is cheaper than marble, capable of taking a high polish, and so naturally spotty that it takes ordinary kitchen fall-out in its stride. It comes in pink and brown overall tones, as well as the more familiar gray.

The most universally popular surface for kitchen floors is hand-made tiling, of the sort imported from Portugal, Provence and Mexico, in heather-mixture shades of great subtlety. As well as bringing a welcome glow to any kitchen, these tiles are less tiring to stand on than stone flags. Earthenware, glazed and unglazed, looks and feels warmer and more sympathetic than stone, though not quite as friendly as wood.

Bricks, laid on their side in herringbone or basket-weave designs, make a cheaper floor than tiles and provide the same warm colour and texture, but it must be said that they are a great deal more porous and difficult to keep clean. A tablespoonful of lye or caustic soda added to the mop bucket lifts out grease and grime noticeably, but you will find that your mop will fall to pieces sooner.

Unglazed quarry tiles, which come in pleasant buff as well as reddish shades, make a good-looking and reasonably inexpensive work surface, edged with a wooden fillet. They can be sealed in order to make them stain-resistant, but personally I prefer them left in their natural state and scoured clean regularly.

Tiles, plain or decorative, come into their own as splashbacks to working surfaces. A patchwork of old decorated tiles looks wonderful, even a few distributed among plain coloured ones add colour and character, but bear in mind that old tiles are considerably thicker than their modern counterparts and plan the tiling to take account of this.

For the majority of kitchen surfaces and purposes, wood is still most people's first choice,

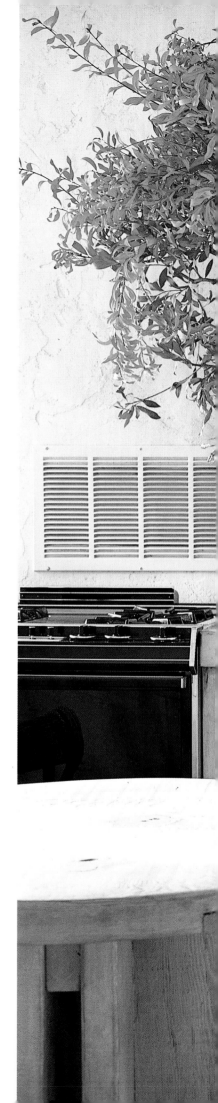

though today massive wooden countertops on cupboards of painted medium-density fibreboard are an affordable compromise. Wood is adaptable and friendly, it deadens the clatter of cutlery and whirring gadgets, it scrubs to an ivory pallor, or can be sealed, waxed or stained.

A wide range of woods can be used as surfaces in the kitchen. Some are chosen for practical reasons – end-grain of beech is hard enough for a chopping block – others on aesthetic grounds – the driftwood look of limed oak is currently a favourite.

Tongue-and-groove or plank walls create a cosy, practical working environment, as well as offering an invitation to decorate with pans, shelves, bygones, baskets or whatever. To secure things onto a wooden wall all you need do is punch a hole in the surface with a bradawl and screw in a couple of hooks.

Where they aren't lined with tiles or wood, walls in country kitchens are usually painted in a plain colour, sometimes with a frieze of stencilled or hand-painted decoration running around just below the ceiling. With painted walls, freshness is all-important in a kitchen context. Take on board country habits and, as in the old limewashed cottage kitchens, scrub down your walls and apply a new coat of paint each spring.

Sumptuous textures in a Californian kitchen, where minimalism turns unexpectedly friendly. Nearly everything is neutral, putty colour – floor tiles, dried plants, driftwoody furniture – but set against plain white, roughcast walls. The sleek black and chrome appliances slot elegantly between cupboards of thick, textured wood. The furniture's chunky shapes belie its sophisticated construction and subtle distressed finish (wipe-on, wipe-off water-based colour) which turns everything silvery, like driftwood. Note that the wood only looks rough hewn; examined closely, all surfaces are honed smooth, not a splinter visible.

THE HEARTH

By one of those ironies which make social history so fascinating, the most primitive cooking arrangement, the open fire on a hearth, has become the height of luxury in gourmet country kitchens. Pampered appetites respond to the pleasures of indoor barbecue food, whether it is potatoes buried in hot ashes, meat sizzled on an iron skillet or chestnuts roasted on a shovel. Some people, blessed with a roomy hearth which once held a cast-iron range, install spits, Dutch ovens and other archaic but effective aids to open-fire cookery. Just the sight of live flames snapping and flickering in a kitchen seems to rouse appetites.

Fashion has come full circle so that an open hearth with a pile of blazing logs seems more of a luxury in the kitchen than the latest thing in fan-boosted wall-mounted electric ovens or a stainless steel rotisserie. These are two exceptionally pleasing examples, one Scandinavian, one English. On the right a classic fish painting over the mantel contrasts with a simple but effective stencilled wall treatment. Below, an antique cast iron fireback – perhaps original to the house – has been set into the chimney, making an unusual decorative feature.

When renovating old kitchens most people tuck the stove away in the hearth space because this does away with the need for a hood, as well as saving space. However, if you can, it is worth finding some other location for your stove, thus leaving the fireplace intact, as it is the greatest treat imaginable to be able to eat beside a real fire. My ideal is a log fire – it will burn down slowly to a heap of white ash and meantime the atmosphere is balsamic. And food that has been cooked over scented logs like hickory or apple wood, or else on great bundles of dried herbs and brushwood, tastes wonderfully authentic.

—RANGES AND—
STOVES

*Far left: The impractical antique
beauty of an old blackleaded range
(bottom) contrasts with the classic
practicality of restaurant equipment
(top).*

*Left: Many country kitchen owners
select either the Rayburn (top), or the
king of cast-iron ranges, the Aga
(bottom).*

Many country kitchens are served by old-fashioned ranges that warm the room as well as the food. A country kitchen without its cast-iron range beaming out warmth always feels a little incomplete, like a temple minus its genial presiding Buddha.

With trifling exceptions, such as the chromed finish on Rayburn hotplate covers, the basic design of these traditional stoves doesn't change with the years. However, the fuel that

*Below: An old cream-enamelled
Rayburn solid fuel range fairly oozes
cottagey charm when dressed up as
here with a broiderie anglaise ruffle
on the mantelshelf, a bright wool rug
and bunches of dried flowers. The
aluminium scuttle is used to transport
coal from store room to kitchen.
Wintertime visitors head straight for
the Windsor chair.*

they burn does; these days only the sentimental or the hard-up need shovel solid fuel – gas-, electric- or oil-fired ranges look after themselves.

Modern built-in cooking equipment is no substitute for the special qualities of these old-style cookers, although if you install a range you may find that a microwave or small electric oven tucked out of sight is a godsend on occasions.

Having lived with a solid fuel range, in both cases a Rayburn, for half my life, I know their delights and their shortcomings intimately. Rayburns are the poor relations of the Aga; indeed, most old cooking stoves are poor relations of that splendid Swedish invention which hums like a contented dragon in so many fortunate modern and not-so-modern country kitchens. But the poor relations are not to be despised. Less thoroughly insulated, they actually give off more heat into the room; though in the long run the Aga, being so much bigger, creates its own benign warmth. The only warm spot in a stone 18th-century Swedish castle I visited was the echoing, cavernous kitchen presided over by an Aga.

My own kitchen is not always the warmest place in my brick Regency house, because, like people, solid fuel ranges go up and down – lacklustre in the morning, thrumming with radiant heat by lunchtime, needing tickling up and feeding to hot up for cooking purposes by early evening. Given regular attention, any solid fuel stove will give off beneficient warmth and perform well in the slow-cooking department. It may take longer to roast a chicken than your wall-mounted, fan-boosted oven, but the bird will yield to the carving knife like butter, and if you cover the bones and bits with water and leave them in the slow oven overnight they will make a rich broth by morning. Foods rarely burn; pans pushed to the side of the hotplate keep nicely

warm, without the contents sticking or going mushy. Plates accidentally left in the warming oven discolour but do not crack. This helpfulness has led me to think of the range as a friend, overlooking the occasions when it unaccountably sulked and the game paté came out bloody or the soufflé remained a tepid custard.

There are other shortcomings to the solid-fuel range (as opposed to the gas, oil or electric Aga). Drawbacks include the fine dust that it deposits in the kitchen and the fact that you need space outside or in a basement to store its fuel. As well, it is

Left: There is no disputing the fact that the Aga is the lord of the kitchen ranges, handsome enough to stand beside carved plasterwork and under a wall full of oil paintings with perfect aplomb. And the Aga stovepipe disappears discreetly into the wall. Pot stands like the one to the right are now eagerly sought out.

Above: The steady throb of heat from these magnificent stoves-cum-room-warmers draws animals like a magnet – a dozing cat in this instance.

unpredictable in the cooking department. I am not ashamed to reveal that I have an Aga on order; cookery writers have trouble living down half-cooked dishes. But I know that the departure of the Rayburn, a 1950s model in pale blue with black, will be like a death in the family. I shall remember, with rueful affection, the times that I crept down in the night for a cup of tea and slipped gratefully into its radiant, enveloping welcome, which always drives off shivers and warms the toes.

In complete contrast to the traditional appearance of old, even antique, ranges, are the utterly functional modern restaurant-quality ranges. In heavy-duty stainless steel and gas-fired, these sturdy pieces of equipment have made a transition in recent years from the professional kitchen into the homes of serious cooks. The American Wolf and Vulcan ranges and the La Cornue ranges from France epitomize these stylish yet practical cookers. Designed for chefs working under pressure, they have all sorts of time-saving and thoughtful features such as flat-top burners which allow heavy pans to be slid across easily and safely, a solid plate shelf and insulated ovens with full-width doors on heavy-duty hinges. One La Cornue model features the best of both worlds, as it incorporates both gas and electric burners and ovens.

Tough-looking, utterly functional, these professional ranges have an integrity which makes them much more suitable for a country kitchen than the latest shiny slot-in oven and cooktop. The stainless steel range shares one feature with the Aga – a comforting durable style; in both cases there is nothing flimsy about the finish or construction. Designed to last, such ranges may seem costly, but they are a sensible investment in the long run as they will outlive umpteen modern built-in oven and hob or cooktop combinations.

SINKS
—AND DRAINERS—

The appeal of the traditional sink to anyone who has struggled to clean a roasting pan in one of the daintily enamelled, shallow, circular modern versions, most of which are not much larger than a soup plate, is its generous, engulfing size.

Installed with solid teak draining boards either side, slightly canted, the large white porcelain sink which so many country kitchens feature is a survival of a more spacious age. It is too spacious, though, for most purposes; I hardly know of any old sink of this sort which does not have a humble plastic bowl sitting inside it in order to make the experience of washing up (not all country kitchens have dishwashers) or peeling potatoes something less than total immersion to the elbow.

Far left: Old-fashioned porcelain sinks are enjoying a revival in nostalgic country kitchens. This unusual double "pot" sink is fed by two separate pairs of brass taps or faucets.

Above: New-fangled stainless steel sinks take second place to more traditional materials like stone, glazed pottery or marble in the updated country kitchen.

Right: A pot sink on plastered piers has a roomy cubbyhole beneath that is just the right spot for a massive terracotta pot. Grooved teak drainers have been installed either side of the sink, with a tiled splashback behind.

Left: Another way to install a pot sink is to site it beneath a solid wood drainer cut to fit exactly and well-sealed to stop water running down behind.

One other drawback to the old-fashioned glazed sink is the acute difficulty of caulking the cracks where sink meets drainer, so that soapy water does not rush down the back and sides to play havoc with the cupboard space beneath. From examples shown in this book, two facts emerge; the drainer should be cut to overhang the perimeter of the sink by a fraction, and below there should be, ideally, a sensible splash-proof open space, rather than a cupboard.

However, the few disadvantages are outweighed by the practical advantages of the ease with which large items such as oven trays can be cleaned, and by their sheer beauty. Anyone who has inherited a kitchen with an old, original sink and drainer like the rugged stone and marble ones shown on

Left, top to bottom: A superb brass tap with china handles is the proper faucet for this old-fashioned pot sink, with its grooved wooden draining boards. Teak needs daily scouring, but makes a kindly surface on which glass and china can safely bounce.

The same traditional arrangement as above, but this time made entirely of marble. This may appear luxurious, but in Mediterranean countries a marble surface may well cost less than a wooden one.

Granite and pique-aisette *tiles form a splashback and mount for a functional lever-operated design. Primitive but sculpturally handsome, this New England sink is made of a single solid slab of granite.*

Top right: Heavy traditional sinks lend themselves to cubbyholes rather than cupboards, as this American example shows.

Bottom right: The kitchen sink turns Palladian with miniature applied Corinthian pilasters, fielded panels and a distinguished, 18th century style finish in "drab" paint, toning successfully with the putty-marbled floor squares. The lively antique wire baskets in various sizes are French, and a charming adjunct to any kitchen.

these pages would naturally be loath to rip out such handsome relics.

Some people enjoy washing up and install their sink under a window so that the leisurely and theraputic dunking of crocks can be combined with checking on the state of the garden or the weather, with bird-watching or merely day-dreaming (a country cook's version of synergy). People who prefer to delegate to a dishwasher should bear in mind how noisy these appliances can be, forcing a quiet chat over morning coffee up to a sustained shout.

From the point of view of efficiency, hygiene and easy maintenance it would be hard to improve on the standard double sink arrangement in stainless steel. These can be humanized to look more friendly in a rustic-style kitchen by choosing a pair of bowls without drainers and setting them into a chunky counter-cum-drainer in solid wood – preferably teak, because it can take endless sousing without warping, cracking or going soggy.

The right choice of tap or faucet for an old-fashioned sink is important. The swivelling mixer variety we know and love today is not necessarily the ideal partner as it can create an undesirable amount of splashing. A pair of individual taps or faucets in solid antiqued brass, wall-mounted, with a tiled surround, will work better and look quite in keeping.

Today, every architectural antique dealer or salvage yard stocks a selection of characterful old taps or faucets, from giants capable of filling a bath in seconds, to pretty little imported versions with the special charm of lettering in French.

Before buying old taps or faucets you should make sure that their size and bore is compatible with today's modern, usually plastic, pipes. A good plumber should be able to sort out problems with obsolete fittings, at a price, but the less dedicated tradesman is likely to either bodge up something shortlived and unsatisfactory or else pocket a call-out fee and then refuse to handle the job. Antique fittings can be very appealing and atmospheric, with their ceramic knobs, brass levers and other refinements, but my advice would be if in doubt, don't. Fittings that don't perform as they should are a perpetual irritation. Besides, the market today is well-catered for by reproduction taps or faucets that have all the advantages of modern technology combined with Victorian or Art Deco styling in chrome, steel or brass finishes. The latter is most common, since to contemporary eyes brass looks too good to cover up with chromium plate.

As between unpolished brass and shiny chrome, I would go for the chrome, which needs no polish to keep it bright, on the basis that life is too short for polishing. But some people enjoy buffing and burnishing brass, finding nothing more quietly redolent of domestic order than an array of gleaming brasswork.

The best tip I know for cleaning up really filthy old brass is to soak it in a vinegar solution for 24 to 48 hours, or until the worst of the gunge has been eaten away. Then rinse off the solution and dry the item. After that, it is a case of applying old-fashioned brass polish, clean rags and elbow grease. Some see working up a radiant gleam on tarnished brass as a sort of spiritual exercise, inculcating a proper pride and attentiveness to detail; certainly there are worse ways of working off surplus energy.

Cheats can make use of the buffer attachment on an electric drill, but I am not fond of that other time-saver's manoeuvre, which is to coat the well-polished object with clear lacquer. The true connoisseur of a properly polished bit of brass will never accept the spurious glitter of lacquered metal in place of the real thing.

—TABLES AND—
CHAIRS

The choice of a kitchen table is usually dictated by how much space is available, what shape it is, and whether the table needs to double as a worktop or counter. Choose a wood that suits your kitchen – English oak, French cherrywood, American maple or universal pine.

A round table on a pedestal base makes a civilized place for family meals and can accommodate extra guests without everyone feeling cramped. Round tables can snuggle into awkward spaces and chairs can be pushed under the top between meals, releasing floor space.

In a tiny space a gateleg table offers flexible seating for between two and eight people, depending on how many flaps are lifted.

The standard pine kitchen table, with a cutlery drawer at each end, has a sturdy simplicity which is perfectly at home in a

Left: Today, country kitchens are furnished, for the most part, with a jumble of old pieces, not all of which began life there. The Windsor chairs shown here, however, are kitchen classics.

Below: Stick-back chairs, a pine settle and a scrubbed deal table furnish a typical English country kitchen, where the children's paintings decorating the walls are as natural as a jug of garden flowers.

country kitchen. A daily scrub with a cream cleanser keeps the top as pale as parchment – just the right background to flatter simple pottery and country food. One drawback can be their height; the older ones are often a little higher than the standard 30 inches

Country furniture is often austerely plain, like this narrow refectory-style table flanked by simple benches. The built-in dresser has been painted a glossy green to contrast with the butter-coloured walls.

(1000 mm) because they were intended to be used by a cook who was standing up. Chopping the legs down is a possible solution, but be careful – if the frame is deep, people won't be able to get their knees under it when sitting.

Where there is space to spare, a long, polished refectory-style table has a generous air. The most attractive antique versions are 19th-century French; they are lighter and more graceful than their English or American counterparts.

A genuine Baptist church pew provides plenty of seating along one side of a modest kitchen table frame topped with salvaged floorboards. The sturdy chairs are in a country Chippendale style.

Sets of chairs are so prohibitively expensive when they have what antique dealers call "a bit of age" that most people opt for the harlequin solution, combining different chairs of roughly the same height, colour or period. A collection of stickback chairs, for

Above: This solid wooden table top was craftsman-made from salvaged maple. Note the practical cutlery drawers built into the frieze. Almost a set, the five stickback chairs are supplemented by a pair of curly bentwood ones.

Right: An antique American table, decorated with a long woven rag runner. With age, the chairs and table have darkened to a rich molasses brown.

Two approaches to furnishing eating areas. The informal kitchen nook focuses around a curious little table made from one thick slice of tree trunk. The Mexican chairs are painted in different bright colours and a further wild contrast is the wonderfully eccentric little buffet table on the left. The main dining space is more restrained, its outrageousness confined to the colourful twiggy infrastructure of a quite ordinary dining table.

instance, always looks handsome, however variously detailed.

Rush-seated chairs are tougher than caned ones and almost as light and portable. Their frames can be considerably enlivened with paint; coloured marbling in the Scandinavian rococo style looks unexpected and pretty. If you can't find a set of antique versions, modern rush-seated chairs, often imported from Portugal, are worth consider-

ing as they retain a gutsy peasant simplicity. The grandeur of upholstered chairs can be toned down by making rustic slipcovers that fall to the floor in either a plain, lightweight canvas or duck or a simple checked cotton.

As an alternative to chairs, against a wall, a high-backed settle can be both distinguished and suitably countrified. And it has a practical advantage; it will seat a surprising number of people.

STORAGE

The problems of storage used to be the subject of endless pages in kitchen design manuals. They went with the built-in kitchen, it seems, with its crafty slots for trays and chopping boards, its swivelling counter-top platform for the food processor, its marble pastry slab neatly inset into a work-top or counter, its oversized pan drawers on special runners, its carousel or lazy susan for corner cupboards. Today's more relaxed approach to kitchen design has a solution to all these problems – that is to let it all, or as much as possible of it, hang out.

People have rediscovered the sheer good looks of most traditional cooking equipment, from enamelled colanders to stoneware bread crocks, and realized that it was a pity, as well as a waste of time, to hide it all away behind faceless banks of cupboards. Besides which, the preparing and cooking processes seem to run more smoothly when the neccessary equipment and gadgets are visible and to hand.

There is no need to overdo things; kitchens

Above: A walk-in pantry with substantial shelving is something of a dream today, though more easily come by in country kitchens. Used as an all-purpose store room, cold room, wine store, a place like this relieves the pressure on kitchen storage.

Below left: This higgledy-piggledy storage system involves a regiment of little cupboards, racks, shelves and suchlike that act as base for an assortment of cooking extras – spice and herb jars, a quiverful of wooden spoons, eggcups, ladles.

Below right: The sort of thing that works best in hot climates, this free-form plastered concrete storage system takes an enormous variety of kitchen equipment and crockery.

Right: Shaker-style peg rails (see p.52) sensibly suspend a flexible choice of shelving from the wall.

where everything – from china to glass, storage jars to gadgets – is displayed on open shelving require constant cleaning and meticulous discipline not to look chaotic. A sensible balance should be the aim, with bulky or boring-looking stuff, like mixing bowls, roasting and loaf pans, food processors and coffee grinders, stashed behind closed doors, but the more appealing items in constant use on view and instantly available. Pots and pans are an obvious example – nothing could be more practical than a traditional pot stand, especially when completed by a matching set of professional quality pans in stainless steel or, newer still, anodized aluminium. A stand each side of the range makes a highly satisfying arrangement, as classic as a pair of bay trees either side of a front door.

Many country kitchens have exposed beams that act as ideal catchment areas for colanders, sieves or other items with handles. Use brass hooks as anchorage; extra-large hooks screwed into ceiling beams take care of

your basket collection, as well as the odd salami, bunch of herbs or string of dried chillies. The undersides of baskets are surprisingly decorative. Frying pans can be attractive too, hooked up like a frieze to a rack on the wall above the stove. A simple sliver of steel fixed above a window invites all manner of attractive ladles and other objects fixed to butcher's hooks.

Sliding baskets on runners make a fine alternative to drawers for paraphernalia best tidied away – cutlery, chopsticks, dishtowels, rolling pins. No one needs urging to display dry goods, spices or herbs in storage jars on open shelves; these make handsome still lives with the minimum of effort. And accessorizing the dresser with a cherished, colourful motley of painted china and bright pottery – plates, saucers, cups, jugs and a row of teapots marching along the top – brings out more creativity than decorating the Christmas tree. The dresser, even more perhaps than the range, is the altarpiece of contemporary country kitchen life.

Carved fruitwood armoires are the ideal complement, or alternative, to a dresser in a roomy kitchen. Prettily lined, with or without their door panels, they can be used to store or display the "best" china and glass.

Not all country storage solutions require large pieces of furniture – there are lots more smaller scale ad hoc storage ideas shown on these pages, such as compact sets of wall shelves or glazed cupboards and cabinets crammed like a useful mosaic on walls.

One relic of earlier storage systems currently enjoying a totally unexpected lease of life as

Dressers need not be antique, or even complete (top shelves will do), to give their owners a lot of pleasure. They provide an excuse to collect pretty bits and pieces and a place to arrange these prizes to their best advantage. Any set of salvaged shelves can be wall-mounted, as here, with or without a table or cupboards beneath. On balance, painted shelving (below right and opposite) makes a more flattering background to china, but plain wood (below left) probably remains most people's first choice.

an art object is the old-fashioned meat-safe, with perforated metal panels on a wooden frame, sometimes known in America as a pie safe or Hoosier cabinet.

In the days before refrigeration made a clean sweep of such problems, keeping perishable meats sweet and untainted involved a whole battery of preservative measures, such as spicing or salting. But in the short run, the greatest enemy was the common fly zooming in on meats with a hint of gaminess, and rapidly reducing a prime joint to a crawling horror.

As one who has ventured on home curing of ham in a cool but not flyproof cellar, I can vouch for the importance of keeping the item in question inaccessible to flies. Layers of salt and spice may not be enough. The essential adjunct of a cool larder or pantry, before refrigeration, was one of these functional, but oddly decorative cabinets. The plainest were simply wiremesh on a frame, but the more attractive, and currently collectible, incorporated panels of punched tin. The aim of both was to let air flow freely, without admitting flies.

Left: A Pennsylvanian pie safe, the American forerunner of the refrigerator. Punched tin panels in the door kept contents cool and aired, while keeping insects out.

Today, some kitchen designers incorporate these panels in the wooden door frames of a run of base or, more often, wall cabinets. The punched designs are based on traditional motifs such as the dove of peace, the Shaker heart or the hospitable pineapple.

Right, top and middle: One of the most enviable aspects of custom-built kitchen equipment and furniture is the attention to detail, as evidenced by this sliding basket arrangement, housed in the base of a freestanding wooden cupboard. The baskets are used to store vegetables in ideally dark/airy conditions. The basket drawers are beautifully made of wicker with round pulls or handles, and run on smooth wooden frames.

Above: Chicken-wire filling in the door panels of a curvy fronted wood armoire allows the contents to be seen; not always what a cook wants, but in this case, where the cupboard holds beautiful porcelain, a positive advantage. As long as the china is in daily use, dust will not have time to collect on it.

Right: Solid and practical door furniture matters a good deal in a kitchen where doors and drawers are in constant use. Of polished brass, these are both decorative and functional. The strap hinges are sturdier than most, while catches and drawer handles or pulls are simple but good-looking.

In the days when women sat down with their sewing and mending every evening as a regular duty, the menfolk might just have been knocking together a home-made meat-safe using whatever materials were to hand. The crafts produced by country people living a long buggy ride from the nearest town are a tribute to their ingenuity and thrifty habits. One of the most striking objects in the McAlpine Collection of Australian artefacts from the outback is a meat-safe made from a petrol or gas drum mounted on a tripod stand and painted blue.

Punching tin would have been light work in comparison to hacking doors out of the side of a drum; you lay your sheet tin on a board and hammer out holes with a steel punch or sharp nail, making slits with an old chisel. As always, the urge to create something decorative as well as practical led to the punching on meat-safe panels becoming organized into patterns. Such items add a touch of true grit to kitchen decoration, besides providing unusual-looking storage space for non-perishables, now that perishables are stored in the refrigerator.

Above: A shallow 18th century dresser in well-rubbed green paint tucks conveniently into otherwise unused space next to a doorway.

Left: This dresser's glossy green paintwork sets off sturdy hand-made pottery in natural browns, buffs and greens. The cookware – casseroles, gratin dishes, jelly moulds – tones with the tableware – plates, teapots and so on.

Above and right: Mahogany graining in a fine, vivid auburn makes a refreshing change from stripped pine. This dresser acts as a dramatic showcase for pottery that is as roaringly colourful as the proverbial flowerbed.

Below: Classic pine is the perfect home for delicate flowered china.

Above: Rescuing and recycling period fragments to make furniture provides the best of both worlds – fluted pilasters and fielded panels along with deep work surfaces, roomy cupboards and ample shelving.

Below: Almost any sturdy cupboard can be converted into a dresser by adding a set of shelves.

Antique kitchenware makes a decorative display arranged on a mellow old dresser. Look for jelly or butter moulds, flour or sugar scoops and shakers and decorative containers for spices or herbs. Your collection can be functional too – this assortment of 18th and 19th century pottery and treen is still in regular use today.

COOK'S
—TOOLS—

Equipment does not create a cook, but by making many processes faster and less tiring to carry out, the right tools probably raise standards and tempt amateurs to aim a little higher or experiment a little more. Buying new gadgets or pans is enjoyable – one of the nicest ways to spend money, in my opinion – but my advice to beginners is to start small, with a well-chosen minimum of good-quality tools. Otherwise, it is depressingly easy to acquire cupboards full of electric meat slicers or pasta-making machines which never pay for the space they occupy in terms of how often you use them. Obviously, your personal cooking style will determine what equipment you find most useful; regular cake-makers will get more mileage out of an electric whisk or a mixer than the cook who lives on pasta and salads.

—BATTERIE DE—
CUISINE

There are a few essential tools that feature in every cook's *batterie de cuisine*. As well as the classic items like knives and wooden spoons, you should give certain modern gadgets houseroom. Of these, a heavy, robust, well-designed mixer is probably the most useful, even if you rarely use more than the chopping blade attachment. You should buy the model with the most powerful motor you can afford. As with all power tools, the motor is everything – a good one does the job quicker and less noisily, and will last longer.

When choosing the more traditional tools, bear in mind that no cook can be without a set of sharp knives. Start with two or three sizes – 3-inch (80-cm), 6-inch (150-cm) and 8-inch (200-cm) versions. Choose knives with riveted handles and plain, not serrated, blades that you can put an edge on with a carborundum stone or a steel knife sharpener. A knife that is honed to an edge so fine that it slides through foods will make you feel like a true professional.

As well as some knives, you should also buy a

Above: Stoneware and unglazed ceramics have a natural dignity which makes them ideal for country cooks. The tamali pot is Mexican, while the stoneware jar is American.

Below left: Pots and pans don't have to be burnished copper to look attractive pegged or hooked to the kitchen wall. Black cast-iron is a practical choice as it looks good without polishing.

Right: Cookware doesn't have to match – an unselfconscious mix is natural to country kitchens.

Far right: A serious challenge to the copper-bottomed stainless steel French or Italian cookpans are these American cast aluminium pans. Unlike the stainless steel type, they have the advantage of looking perfectly at home in both modern and traditional-style kitchens.

swivel-bladed peeler to make light work of preparing root vegetables or peeling potatoes. And for heavier tasks, such as jointing chickens or chopping through bones for the stockpot, I recommend one of the weighty cleavers stocked by most Chinese cookshops. These are not stainless steel, but for that reason they can be ground to a finer edge and are inexpensive compared with the best French or Swiss equipment. Chinese cooks use two at a time, and can reduce a heap of vegetables or a mound of parsley to tiny particles in a moment.

Sharp tools are useless without a good chopping surface to work on. De-luxe kitchens have these built into an island unit or worktop counter at the right height. And antique butchers' blocks have become chic chopping boards in many kitchens. The board you choose should be heavy, dense (end grain is best) and large; bread boards are too small and more often than not allow half their load to fly off around the kitchen. On the other hand, a massive board is only

Right: A kitchen sculpture of the unselfconscious kind includes a wooden candle box, an unusual spoon and scoop, a cooking thermometer and an old-fashioned corkscrew that is generous in size.

Below: Antique candle boxes can be adapted to hold 20th century essentials like kitchen paper.

Right: Once upon a time these antique moulds in cast iron would have been put away between baking sessions. Today the decorative potential of these charming pieces is seized upon to make the kitchen version of a silhouette collection. This is a collector's kitchen: note the bunches of baskets on butcher's hooks and the striped china marching across the stove hood.

useful if you are able to keep it out on a surface at all times, handily close to a magnetic rack where you store your knives.

It is perfectly possible, and in the tradition of rustic cooking, to improvize with tools. You can whisk egg whites with a fork, roll out pastry with a bottle, dribble oil into mayonnaise from an old vinegar cruet or small jug. How often you perform these culinary rites and how much storage space you have to spare will dictate whether you should improvize or buy the specific, purpose-made tools for the job. Money is less important as a deciding factor, especially as junk or thrift shops and garage or boot sales are usually well-supplied with old kitchen tools. An old-fashioned wooden rolling pin and a hand-operated egg beater are both worth scouring secondhand sources for.

Good pots and pans are costly – secondhand, you could buy your own vehicle for the price of a set of copper-bottomed stainless steel pans with non-heating handles and a lid that you can pick up without burning your fingers. The best policy is to save up and buy

these one or two at a time. Your first purchase should be two moderately sized pans – a 4-pint (2-litre) and either a 5- or 6-pint (2½- or 3-litre) version for everyday boiling of vegetables, soups and sauces. A 6-pint (3-litre) pan can usually take a colander or round sieve, which, with the lid perched on top, will convert it into a steamer. You should also get a shallow lidded pan or skillet for frying and braising.

People go to enormous trouble to put basic equipment like pots and pans out of sight in

sliding drawers or hung up high from ceiling racks. My own preference in the average-sized kitchen is for a pyramidal pot stand, which makes a practical and handsome adjunct to a stove. Floor-standing ones which take an entire set of pans are ideal if you have enough floor space. If you don't, buy a smaller one which can stand on your work surface close to the cooktop. In white or brightly enamelled cast-iron, these stands always look good – especially if you keep your pans well-scoured – as well as providing convenient access.

For stewing or braising the best equipment is probably a mixture of heavy cast-iron pots with lids and the sort of attractive earthenware stewpots that are imported from France, Spain and Italy. The cast-iron type have the advantage that they can be used on any type of hob or cooktop – gas flame, electric hot plate or Aga – and in any of the matching ovens, though they lose their looks fast over gas rings, becoming blackened and encrusted. Earthenware is cheap and attractive and looks comely enough for the table,

but needs to be "seasoned" (heat a layer of oil in it slowly) and treated with care. Earthenware vessels should only be put over direct heat if an intervening flame tamer (wire mesh mat) is used to diffuse the flame. Also, it is as well to avoid sudden extremes of temperature – moving a pot from the flame onto a cold marble surface for instance, or adding cold liquid to a simmering pot.

Usually glazed inside, unglazed without, and lidded, simple earthenware peasant containers are the most sensuous of all to cook with. They come in a huge variety of shapes and sizes, to suit traditional dishes. Tall beanpots, for instance, narrow toward the top, to reduce evaporation. Stewpots are oval or round, with lids. The oval shape is best for braising birds or rabbit. Many of these dishes are very versatile. Personally, I am very attached to a shallow, round dish, with little handles, in chunky brown earthenware. I use it for cooking and serving gratins, rustic layered dishes (pork, onions, apple and potatoes), polenta, *Pommes Anna* and many more. Occasionally, it is also pressed into service as an impromptu salad bowl.

Just how extensive and how various your collection of ovenware should be is debatable. Patience Gray, in her extraordinarily evocative book, *Honey from a Weed*, suggests that even primitive kitchens need various beanpots, lidded casseroles and unlidded gratin-type dishes, as well as two lidded cast-iron pots – a marmite and an oval casserole. My advice would be to start with one of each sort, or two in different sizes, and see how you go, bearing in mind her adage: "The merit lies not in the possession of the object but in putting it to use."

The above, plus the usual colanders, sieves (two – one round, one conical, for sauces), a family of wooden spoons in various sizes and a spatula or two, make up a reasonably efficient basic *batterie de cuisine*. Of course you

Above: Functional but old-fashioned tools – scales, flour bins, whisks and such like – can be found for a song. Their period charm makes them much more decorative than today's equivalents.

Right: A handcrafted coatrack makes an ideal rail to hang a huge family of metal spoons.

also need bowls for mixing and storing, roasting pans and so forth, but these are minor purchases.

One further item of importance in any kitchen is a really heavy pestle and mortar for pulverizing anything and everything too small or scanty to go through the mixer. Antique versions of this classic culinary tool tend to be the most satisfactory because they are heaviest. Mine, in some form of alloy resembling brass or bell metal, was bought in a camel market in Tunisia along with a big paper bag of what purported to be saffron stigma, dirt cheap. The saffron turned out to be – as I half suspected – largely made up of marigold petals, but the mortar and pestle remain in constant, regular use, clonking melodiously in unison with grinding spice, pesto, black peppercorns or sea salt.

Having laid so much stress on scaling your equipment to your needs and lifestyle, it may seem perverse to urge you to splurge on certain enormous items that you will only use once or twice a year. However, I find that whereas improvization works wonders in most cooking processes, when you need a really huge pan or dish (for boiling hams, or steaming a big steak and kidney pudding or a whole fish), nothing in the average home can substitute. In my time I have tried old metal baths, mop pails and bread bins with unfortunate results like the solder melting. Forget about coppered jelly moulds in the shape of fish or colourful paté dishes with crouching hares for handles – these are mere decoration. Look out instead for one really big pan – a tinned copper preserving pan perhaps, or one of those old-fashioned, enamelled metal roasting pans with a domed, dimpled lid known as a Dutch oven. Given a big enough stove, these are not only excellent for the Sunday roast, but ideal for poaching large fish, simmering a small ham and so on.

Above: A highly personal batterie de cuisine *– a lifetime's collection of wooden spoons and spatulas plus the odd ladle. Bowls act as "nests" for cookie cutters and suchlike small clutter. The logic here is compellingly simple – if you want to stash something where it will be remembered, leave it to hand and it is more likely to be used.*

Left: The trouble with pattypans is finding a place to store them. A sturdy basket keeps them prettily to hand.

Left: An old Spanish container, probably for salt, has found a new life as a home for wooden spoons. Practical country cooks always recycle the old, rather than buy new.

Right: Every country kitchen should have a solid mortar and pestle to pulverize anything and everything that is too small to go into the mixer – spices, pesto or sea salt, for example. Mortar and pestle sets are available in stoneware, as here, or in wood or metals such as brass.

Left: Nutmeg graters have compartments for storing a whole "nut" of spice. Freshly grated nutmeg is much more potent than the ready-grated, powdered type.

Right: Antique carved English wooden bread boards and knives are perfectly at home in a country kitchen setting. Many feature endearing mottoes, such as "Welcome" or "There is no place like home". For hygiene reasons, restrict their use to bread.

Left: Pans can be pressed into use as temporary storage places for perishables that pass through your kitchen – this black enamel one has been used to house a family of shallots.

Right: A painted spoon rack stores an assortment of antique treen scoops. If you can't find an old rack, make one and age it with paint. Practical as well as decorative, these scoops make ideal serving spoons for condiments like salt, sugar, mustard or pepper.

Right: A collection of antique treen – those everyday items carved in wood and worn to a glossy polish through years of handling – can be both beautiful and useful. Store and display things like pegs, butter moulds and tools in wooden bowls or racks.

Left: Carved wooden moulds for impressing patterns on butter or in biscuit or cookie dough are worth collecting. The small two-piece mould shown here is used to make decorative butter pats.

Right: In the days when young men carved and painted wooden spoons as betrothal gifts for their sweethearts, much care went into making little racks to display these family treasures.

Left: Wooden bowls nest comfortably, one inside the other. These examples are antique and Scandinavian, but you can buy modern versions in a wide range of woods. These are either handcrafted in the West or else imported from third-world countries like India.

Right: For a country kitchen table you should choose rustic wooden salad servers, like these early 20th century carved examples, rather than modern plastic ones.

Left: Old-fashioned equipment adds to the pleasure of home-baking. Like the cookie cutters, which are of a traditional American type, the wooden pastry wheel, pottery mixing bowl and Shaker-style flour bin are all still made today.

POTTERY

Earthenware, whether glazed or unglazed, decorated or plain, is everyone's favourite kitchen self-indulgence. In simple traditional shapes and vibrant colours, ceramic wares combine usefulness with homey beauty in a thoroughly satisfying way. People have enjoyed collecting and displaying pottery in their kitchens for hundreds of years, and at every social level, from the goodwife trading eggs, butter and cheeses at market for sturdy slipware in brown and cream, to the 18th century Swedish countess who fitted up her boudoir-cum-kitchen with a clutch of cherub brackets to display her remarkable collection of blue-and-white Chinese export ware.

Just how prized these kitchen gewgaws were can be gauged by the care with which broken pieces were riveted so that the item could

Left and below left: Country themes of animals and flowers decorate this fresh blue and green spongeware, made by the English potters Hinchcliffe and Barber. The design has co-ordinating cotton print tablelinen.

Below right: Plain glazes in rich buttery ochre, sea green and blue are all the decoration this attractive pottery from Provence needs. Food, especially summery salads and seafoods, looks especially appetizing against these colours. This sort of mixed collection from a "family" of ceramics is good to look at and has the advantage that breakages are easier to replace.

start a new life as a wall decoration, somehow more appropriate for a kitchen than pictures in frames. Damaged plates and saucers turn up quite frequently and their "faultiness" is reflected in the price. A group of these on a kitchen wall makes the prettiest flowery splash of colour.

Antique or merely old pottery gets rarer all the time, although bargains have a way of surfacing in the unlikeliest places. Attractive pieces tended to travel, perhaps as voyager's souvenirs or presents bought home by sailors for their mothers or sweethearts. This may be why brilliant Moorish tiles can turn up in Norway or Quimper ware from Brittany materialize in Edinburgh. If the price is not scandalous, opportunities like these should be seized because they are becoming fewer

and further between. One or two older pieces mixed in with modern ones gives dignity to the whole collection.

Functional native pottery – ranging from unglazed gratin dishes to brightly glazed serving bowls – is invariably cheaper bought on its own territory. Avoid tourist shops and follow the local inhabitants' practice of stocking up at street markets. Except for one occasion, when a Portuguese slipware platter came to pieces trundling through the airport X-ray equipment, I have never regretted my impulse buys, however cumbersome.

Spongeware has a popular appeal, whether in bright green and white from Italy or soft

Right: The Mexican love of bright colour and vivid patterns inspires pottery designs that are as brilliant as a bunch of zinnias. Painting the insides of china cupboards in a definite colour, a warm terracotta was used here, shows up the colours and textures. The vivid pottery is teamed with hand-made glass from the same region, in rich shades of deep green and cranberry red.

pastels from England. Studio potters like Hinchcliffe and Barber produce the most inventive spongeware, often with designs of fishes or fruit imposed over a sponged background. Their ceramic is heavier and of finer quality than the mass-produced sort and inevitably more expensive. All these potteries create new designs frequently and anyone with a dresser to fill should have no difficulty building up a wonderfully colourful show. If you plan to collect sets of one design only it is sensible to check whether it will remain in production, and for how long.

As well as these relatively mass-produced designs, there are scores more small potteries

turning out one-offs or limited ranges of mugs or jugs in a number of glazes and finishes; these are always worth investigating as any one of them could turn out to be tomorrow's Lucie Rie.

However strongly you may feel that pretty things should be used and take their chances, rather than gather dust in a cupboard, the "best" china, delicately hand-painted and touched with gold and lustre, is too precious for daily use in country kitchens. Breakages are just too hard to forgive, and then you can't forgive yourself for minding.

Anyone fortunate enough to own a spectacular dinner service as well as a spacious

kitchen in the manor-house style might consider, instead, turning the dining area (see page 43) into a modern version of the stately home "china closet". Line the walls with purpose-made shelving, carefully designed. The proportions must be right for the china, some form of concealed lighting should be installed to show the collection off after dark, and the shelves must have some depth so that you aren't liable to brush off items in passing.

Generally speaking, china closets have closed cupboards up to dado level, for storing odds and ends or the second-best china, and open shelving above that height which reaches to

within a foot or so of the ceiling. This allows you to stand large pieces on top, rather in the manner of busts in a library. Some people cage in the shelving with chickenwire or brass mesh, while others prefer glazed doors to the display shelves. The paint colours used for the inside of the shelving must be chosen to set off the decoration on the china as attractively as possible. Tinted glazes usually create the most satisfactory colours for the purpose, as they are clear and clean without being too bright. The paint selected for the exterior joinery should take its cue from the shelving colour, with dark shades – green, black, mahogany graining – in the lead.

Right: Country tableware is not always paintbox bright; this serenely plain pottery and glassware has a new rustic, green simplicity. Everything in this cupboard is basic yet beautiful – from the solid salvaged wood shelving to the greenish tumblers of recycled glass. Even the pottery is eco-conscious; harmful substances are kept to an absolute minimum, with only the insides of the pieces glazed.

However, the altogether more informal air of the average country kitchen is usually better suited to less valuable pottery – either a job lot collected over the years, or a set of one of the many colourful designs on the market today. Perhaps the ideal is to have a bit of both; a collection of old pieces for show, and for the fun of adding to it, plus an easily replaceable set for everyday use.

Old pottery tended to be decorated crudely, but eye-catchingly, in a limited range of strong colours. Like spongeware, spatterware was a popular rustic style. It was produced in quantities in America during the 19th century. And Provençal "marbled"

Below and below right: Old china comes in patterns as varied and pretty as auriculas. Buying odd pieces is an inexpensive way to build a collection.

ceramics are another striking form of traditional decoration, usually executed in soft browns and creamy yellows. The technique for creating the intricately "marbled" clay base, with two or more coloured clays rolled together before being sliced across like a swiss roll, remains a trade secret in the few potteries which still make these distinctive wares.

Delft, with its decoration in deep blue (and sometimes manganese) on white, remains perhaps the most influential of the antique decorative traditions, and blue and white is probably still the most popular of all colour schemes for domestic ceramics.

Transfer-printed designs which combine printed outlines with splashy hand-painted colour were popular from the 18th century onward, and must have been produced on a mass scale because so many examples survive. I once found and bought half-a-dozen cups and saucers with chinoiserie transfer designs for a trifling price in my local market. Not all have survived, but it encouraged me to look for more of the same; now vastly more expensive, sad to say.

Cost is unfortunately the snag with collecting even these lesser pieces, now that a cup and saucer displayed on a stand is such a popular ornament. However, it is a comforting fact that most old decorated pottery "goes together", so that all sorts of unrelated bits and pieces can add up to a fine show. As with most collections, the thrill of the chase is often just as important as the pride of ownership.

Teapots and mugs are probably the most important kitchen crocks of all, especially in Britain. Most households replace both several times a year, splashing out occasionally on a brighter, jollier or sturdier design.

One of the clever touches that has spurred on the success of Emma Bridgwater's sprightly decorated ceramics, designed with country-style kitchens clearly in mind, was the scaling-down of mugs to 18th century prop-ortions. Bridgwater's squat little cylinders, with their flat bases and comfortable, gener-ous loop handles, are pleasant to use and contain tea and coffee in modest quantity. One 18th-century quality which few modern ceramics can equal, sadly, is resilience or strength. I have a little lustre mug, probably dating from the late 18th century, which has seen out regiments of brand-new versions.

I have often wondered over the abundance of antique teapots to be found in antique markets, until it struck me recently that this phenomenon is directly linked to the growing – and to my mind disastrous – popularity of teabags over the loose-leaf variety. Without being precious, it strikes me as difficult to enjoy teabag tea, which in the main tastes of tannin and dust. Yet in tea-loving Britain, the supermarket chains are reported to be phasing out loose-leaf tea in favour of teabags.

Still, if this releases yet more eccentric, exotic or merely pretty old teapots onto the market, some of us will be gainers. I find a row of old teapots at least as charming as a row of old jugs on shelves and dressers; though it is true that their spouts are vulnerable to damage. But then, their selection of designs is so engagingly quirky that I can overlook the odd chipped spout. I have found bamboo-style pots, teapots shaped like animals or fruit, aquiline and snub-nosed versions, Wedgwood teapots in black basalt, as lean and dark as whippets, and delicious old lustre teapots, friendly and squat, glowing invitingly as tarnished pennies.

Ceramic novelties like cow creamers are also worth collecting to decorate dressers and mantelshelves. One of the finest collections of ceramic cow creamers is to be found in the Stoke-on-Trent museum, where immense cases contain herds of cow creamers, in bewildering but decorative variety.

Above and above left: A mix and match collection of modern decorative pottery from the studios of Hinchcliffe and Barber.

CONTAINERS

Containers for food have been made of virtually every material under the sun – from birch bark to beaten brass, woven straw to hollowed gourds. People used what was cheap, available, and suited to their purpose. Food being too precious to waste, such containers were finely and carefully crafted. Their shapes and textures make them into unselfconscious works of art, which are, if anything, improved by being much used and handled. Such pieces include stoneware cider jars, wooden flour bins, egg racks of painted wood or china, and a whole tribe of salt boxes in wood, ceramic and metal, designed to keep this essential condiment dry and handy for the cook.

Antique containers do sometimes turn up relatively cheaply. I bought an 18th century candlebox recently, of oak darkened and polished by age and use, with pretty dovetailing and a carved loop to hang it by. All it lacked was a sliding lid, pencil-box style, and this defect marked down its price. I plan to have a new lid made by a carpenter friend and decorate it with painted motifs borrowed from an early American piece. Restoring or

recycling old items like this is an inexpensive way of adding atmosphere to a kitchen.

Functional antique kitchen pieces, from stoneware jars to saltglaze containers of various sorts, are easy on the pocket and their chunky shapes and restrained colouring make them welcome in any country kitchen. Displayed in quantity, their effect is magnified. I often wish that I had spent more time rootling about in the 19th-century garbage tip some bright schoolboys struck upon when I was living in Dorset, England. Three or four stoneware jars are nice to have, but shelves of them, labelled, add up to much more than the sum of the parts. These old jars have one drawback; they have no lids. I make do with outsize corks.

The idea of suiting receptacle to provider has provided a wealth of amusing ceramic containers over the centuries, from small pieces like nut dishes and bowls decorated with squirrels, leaves and hazel nuts, to large tureens and dishes in the shape of vegetables, fruit and leaves of various sorts. Look for antique or new leaf-shaped dishes in shiny green ceramic, intended to hold fruit,

mayonnaise containers in the shape of lemons sitting on green leaves or asparagus dishes in, quite simply, the shape of a bundle of asparagus tied around with a wisp of grass. All these rustic pieces have enormous decorative potential, whether enlivening spreads of country food or ranged in glazed cupboards or on dresser shelves.

Sets of enamelled or china canisters inscribed with their contents were common all over Europe and America. Choosing a set labelled in another language – *Riz, Riso, Arroz* or *Reis* – is a neat way of introducing a touch of cosmopolitanism to your kitchen.

Far and away the most popular, cheap and practical storage for the majority of foodstuffs is the glass jar. Available in bright blue or cloudy green as well as the ever-popular clear glass, and in a wide range of shapes and sizes, their advantages are self-evident; the main one being that you can recognize the container's contents immediately. Lined up on a set of shelves, the good looks of the foods within – their varied colour, textures and shapes – are made the most of. However, a few substances, like dried herbs, last better if kept in the dark. With these, either store the jars behind cupboard doors or resort to opaque containers.

The other classic and dependably handsome kitchen container with a multitude of uses is the basket, ranging all the way from tiny bowl-shaped ones that hold garlic or nutmegs, to shallow, segmented trays for cutlery or long panniers for bread. In wicker, twig or willow, their presence adds a touch of skilled craftsmanship which is never out of place in the context of a country kitchen. Rediscovered recently are the old wire baskets traditionally used for kitchen storage in France. Light, strong and decorative, stand these on your counter or work surface to make the prettiest holders for eggs, tomatoes and so forth.

Left: Closed containers like the spongeware pot and creamware semolina jar here are best for dry goods that need to be kept in an airtight dark place. Use baskets, bowls and jugs to store more transient produce – apples, bunches of herbs or garden greenery.

Top right: Baskets of all sizes have a myriad of uses for kitchen storage, from bottles and china to vegetables, fruit and eggs. Cutlery need not languish in a drawer – bone-handled knives look charming bundled into a pottery bowl.

Middle right: A pot stand in metal or cast iron will keep pans and pots accessible. Don't ignore the potential of the wall for storage. Usually, items that are only used from time to time – here, large meat plates, carving knife and fork and the key to the clock – are tucked at the back of a cupboard or drawer, forgotten and hard-to-find.

Bottom right: A dairymaid's yoke is a novel alternative to the ubiquitous ceiling rack. Its clutch of baskets hold a miscellany of kitchen clutter. Behind, a small set of shelves display preserves and chutneys within easy reach.

Top row, left to right: A French wire carrier holds everyday glasses; an English willow basket transports a crop of apples; a hand-made sycamore bowl stores and displays local apples; a French wire colander keeps mushrooms fresh.

Middle row, left to right; Pack home-made preserves and pickles into reusable glass jars (top); use small treen containers to store seasonings (bottom); wicker baskets make convenient resting places for squashes or fruit; bowls keep spices to hand – clockwise from top: fenugreek, cinnamon, cumin, paprika and coriander; dishes are useful homes for tools (top) or ingredients (bottom).

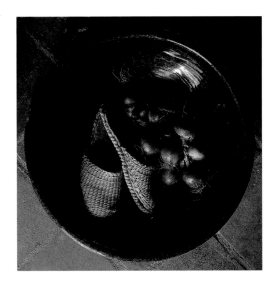

Bottom row, opposite far left and left: Bowls and baskets can be pressed into use for storing perishables; their practical beauty brings a changing series of still-lifes to your kitchen counter.

Bottom row, middle left and middle right: Antique wooden carriers for cutlery or bottles and jars are attractive enough to transport their contents from the work surface to the table.

Bottom row, right and far right: Sturdy stoneware jugs, bowls and pots are dual-purpose; they can be used to store and serve an ever-changing selection of foods.

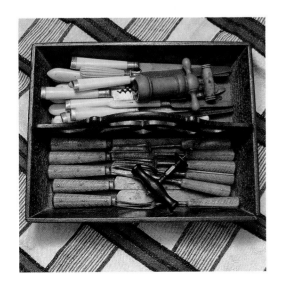

—COUNTRY—
RECIPES

Country food, in the main, is peasant food, reaching back through generations to the daily fare eaten by our farming forebears. This unpretentious food, based on what is available locally and in season, is currently featuring on the menus of sophisticated and adventurous restaurants. Dishes include classics like sausages and polenta, salt cod, thick fish soups, huge fruit tarts with wavy rather than perfect crusts. Squeaky freshness and sizzling immediacy of taste are the qualities we admire and strive for, rather than immaculate platefuls where not a whisker of garnish is out of place. Country cooking is about real food made from fresh ingredients rather than expensive, out-of-season rarities. The rarity that is prized, and appropriate, is of a different sort – freshly gathered vegetables, blackberries or fungi, or newly baked bread.

SOUPS

Garbure

A hearty, well-flavoured, regional French dish. The result will be something between a thick soup and a liquid stew, depending on how much water or stock you add. The basic ingredients should be navy (haricot) beans, cabbage and some form of pork – I have used pork belly and smoked shoulder butt (boiling bacon) successfully. A garlic sausage ring improves the flavour too. A selection of vegetables can be added, chosen according to season. Traditional are green beans, fava (broad) beans, turnips and carrots. The French serve this "soup" poured over slices of bread. The meat is usually eaten separately, but you may prefer to chop it into chunks and serve it in the soup, as here. Serves 4.

1 cup dried navy beans (8 oz/225 g haricot beans, cubed)
1 turnip, diced
2 carrots, diced
2 celery stalks, sliced
1½ cups cubed potatoes (8 oz/225 g potatoes, cubed)
1 pound (1 lb/450 g) pork belly or 1 piece boiling bacon
1 garlic sausage ring
2-3 cloves garlic, crushed
thyme and/or marjoram
salt and pepper
water or stock
1 cabbage, shredded
1 cup sliced green beans (4 oz/100 g green beans, sliced)

Soak the navy (haricot) beans in water to cover overnight. Drain, put them in a pan with fresh cold water to cover and bring slowly to a boil. Simmer, covered, for 45 minutes-1 hour.

Add the turnip, carrots, celery and potatoes, meat, with the garlic, herbs, salt and pepper. If you have any stock, add it to the bean water. Simmer for 1 hour, skimming off any scum as it rises in the pan. Now add the cabbage and green beans. Mix all the ingredients together and cook for another 30 minutes-1 hour.

Provençal soup with pistou

This is a simple, solid sort of soup, halfway to a vegetable stew. It is based on a clutch of new season's vegetables, as fresh and young as possible, simmered together in plain water with a handful of rice to thicken and a handful of noodles for substance. The heady aromatic *pistou*, stirred in at the moment of serving, brings the dish to life. In Provence a sprinkling of grated cheese is often added for quick protein. Serves 4.

Soup:
2 tablespoons olive oil
½ cup (3½ oz/90 g) rice
1 large onion, chopped
½ pound (8 oz/225 g) seasonal vegetables: green beans, trimmed and cut in half; fava (broad) beans, hulled; peas, hulled; zucchini (courgettes) cut into matchsticks
3-4 new carrots, scraped
4 new potatoes, scrubbed and sliced
½ cup chopped fresh pasta (2 oz/50 g fresh pasta, broken into short lengths)
salt and pepper

Pistou:
3-4 cloves garlic
3-4 sprigs of basil
1 tablespoon pignoli (pine kernels)
1 tablespoon fruity olive oil
½ lemon

An earthenware casserole makes the ideal pot to cook this soup in, stood over a flame tamer (wire mat) to diffuse the heat. Otherwise use an enamelled cast-iron pot. Heat the oil gently over low heat and add the rice and onion, turning them in the oil until the onion softens a little. Add all the prepared vegetables and stir around until they are oily and hot, taking care not to let them scorch. Pour over hot water to cover and bring to a boil, then clap on the lid and cook fast for 10 minutes.

Meanwhile, make the *pistou* by simply reducing the ingredients to a fine paste, either by pounding in a mortar or by whizzing in a blender or food processor. (If you use a blender or processor you may need to add more oil to lubricate the blades). Set the *pistou* aside.

Drop the pasta into the pan with the vegetables and cook until *al dente* – 3-5 minutes. Add salt and pepper to taste. Now stir in the *pistou*, stand for 1-2 minutes to let the aromatics mingle, then serve in shallow bowls.

Leek and potato soup

I feel that savoury country soups should be halfway to a meal, eaten with bread and cheese. Tasty and generous, rather than *recherché*, they all share in common the use of familiar, local foodstuffs. The quantity below serves 4.

½ stick (2 oz/50 g) butter
3 cups cubed potatoes (1 lb/450 g potatoes peeled and cubed)
5 cups sliced leeks (1¼ lb/575 g leeks, trimmed and sliced)
1 lettuce or 2 heads Belgian endive (chicory), chopped
a handful of fresh herbs such as parsley, basil and savory
5 cups (2¼ pints/1.25 litres) hot chicken or beef stock
salt and pepper

Melt the butter over a low heat in a deep cast-iron or earthenware pan. Add the chopped prepared vegetables and herbs and sweat, turning frequently until softened a little. Pour on the hot stock, cover and simmer for 1 hour, or until everything is tender and the potatoes are beginning to break up. Add salt and pepper to taste.

Left: Garbure, top, Provençal soup with pistou, middle, and Leek and potato soup, bottom, served in chunky Provençal earthenware. Soups can be cooked in earthenware pots like these as long as a flame tamer (wire mat) is used to diffuse the heat. Parmesan cheese (shown in the foreground) can be grated over servings of the Provençal soup.

Iced sorrel soup

Sorrel gives a wonderful tang to this summer soup, but young spinach leaves may be used instead if your garden does not run to this vegetable. Serves 4.

1 cucumber, peeled and chopped

1 bunch sorrel leaves, torn into strips

1 clove garlic

4 scallions (spring onions), finely chopped

4¾ cups (2 pints/1.1 litres) chicken stock

⅔ cup light cream (¼ pint/150 ml single cream)

salt and pepper

fresh chives, parsley, chervil or tarragon to garnish

Place cucumber, sorrel, garlic and scallions (spring onions) in a large pan with the chicken stock and bring to a boil. Simmer until the cucumber and scallions (spring onions) are soft.

Let the mixture cool somewhat, then whizz until smooth in a food processor or blender. Stir in the cream and mix thoroughly. Add salt and pepper to taste. Serve chilled with a few herbs sprinkled over.

Gazpacho

Although red-hot in colour and highly spiced, this Spanish soup is served ice-cold. This quantity feeds 4.

2 slices bread, diced

1 tablespoon oil

1 clove garlic, crushed

¼ cucumber, peeled and diced

½ small onion, peeled and diced

1 tomato, peeled and diced

1 pound (1 lb/450 g) tomatoes, peeled

1 large onion

2 cloves garlic

1 green pepper

½ cucumber, peeled

1 can tomato juice

cayenne pepper to taste

2-3 tablespoons lemon juice

4-6 tablespoons olive oil

Fry the bread cubes in the oil and garlic. Reserve the resulting croutons, with the diced cucumber, onion and tomato, to serve with the soup.

Purée the tomatoes, onion, garlic, pepper and cucumber and mix with the tomato juice and cayenne pepper. Add the lemon juice and olive oil a little at a time, tasting frequently to make sure that the soup is neither too sharp nor too oily. Chill well.

Serve in individual bowls with an ice cube floated on top. Fill side dishes with the diced vegetables and croutons.

Cold cherry soup

A fruit soup makes a refreshing start to a meal. The rich colour of the cherries ensures that this one looks as good as it tastes. Serves 4.

13½ cups (4½ lb/2 kg) black or morello cherries

3 cloves

½ teaspoon cinnamon

1 cup (8 oz/225 g) sugar

half a bottle of red wine

2½ cups (1 pint/600 ml) water, boiled and cooled

2 tablespoons sour cream to garnish (optional)

With a mallet, crush the cherries and some of their stones. To get a thicker, quicker result you could pit the cherries, then blend in a food processor.

Leave the cherry purée in an earthenware bowl with the spices and the sugar for a few hours to draw the juices. If you crushed the cherries you will need to put them through a coarse sieve to remove the remaining stones.

Mix in the wine and dilute with water to taste. Serve chilled, with maybe a dollop of sour cream.

Right: Cold cherry soup, top, and Iced sorrel soup, bottom, served in summery faience bowls. The sorrel soup is garnished with chives and the cherry soup with flat-leaved parsley.

-SPREADS AND-
PATES

Terrine of rabbit and fruit from Alsace

Lean and tender rabbit, whether wild or farmed, is becoming a serious alternative to chicken with the modern generation of chefs. It has always featured in country cookery; a rabbit for the pot being easy to come by as a rule. Ask your supplier to skin and paunch the rabbit, setting aside the liver separately. If one large rabbit is unavailable, buy two smaller ones.

This is an unusual, elegant terrine, good for a buffet or family feast. It should be kept for several days to allow the flavours to develop, so start making it a week ahead of time.

1½ pounds (1½ lb/675 g) streaky pork, not too fat
a handful of sea salt
3 pound (3 lb/1.4 kg) rabbit – 1 large or 2 small
about 6 tablespoons calvados, marc, or cognac
2 teaspoons salt
1 teaspoon green or black peppercorns
1 carrot
1 small onion
1 stick celery
1 bouquet garni
2-3 tablespoons corn oil
1 egg
1 cup (8 oz/225 g) chopped firm greengages or damsons, pitted and chopped
2-3 sprigs of fresh thyme

Garnish:
nasturtium or borage flowers
watercress

Pork is greatly improved by overnight salting to remove some of its water content. Strip the rind off the meat, then rub a handful of salt – *gros sel* or sea salt is best – well in, all over. Leave in a cool place, or in the refrigerator.

Strip all the meat off the rabbit carcass with a very sharp knife, setting aside some fine pieces whole. Turn the meat into a bowl with half the alcohol, the salt and the peppercorns. Cover and marinate in the refrigerator overnight.

The next day, rinse and wipe the pork, cut it into small pieces and add to the rabbit marinade. Leave overnight. Chop the rabbit bones across. Put them in a large pan, with the carrot, onion, celery, bouquet garni and water to cover. Bring to a boil, then lower the heat and simmer until well reduced. (There should be about 1 cup/8 fl oz/250 ml.) Strain and set aside.

Pick out the best bits of the rabbit meat and its liver. Heat the oil in a pan and sauté these pieces of meat lightly until stiffened. Sprinkle over the remaining alcohol and leave to cool.

Chop the remaining rabbit meat and pork finely together. This can be done most easily in a food processor, efficiently with an old-fashioned grinder (mincer), and satisfactorily with a sharp cleaver. Indeed, purists would argue that meats chopped by hand with a razor-edged cleaver remain juicier, with more texture. Turn the chopped meat into a large bowl and beat in the egg and reserved stock, then the chopped fruit. Chop the lightly cooked liver, add it to the bowl and mix thoroughly.

Oil a 3-pound (3-lb/1.4-kg) terrine and lay 1 sprig of thyme on the base. Half fill with the meat mixture, then lay the lightly cooked rabbit morsels across. Pack in the remaining meat mixture and finish with another sprig of thyme. Cover with foil and a lid, and place the terrine in a roasting pan. Add boiling water to a depth of 1 inch (2.5 cm) and bake in a 350°F (180°C/Gas Mark 4) oven for 1½ hours. The terrine is cooked when it starts to shrink away from the sides of the container and feels firm and springy. Leave to cool.

Eat after 4 or 5 days, turned out on a plate and garnished with nasturtium or borage flowers and watercress.

Left: Terrine of rabbit and fruit from Alsace, served on hand-potted stoneware. A salad of tomatoes and oak-leaved lettuce accompanies the terrine.

Tapenade

Tapenade is a sort of relish, salty and pungent, much eaten in Provence, France. You can spread it on toast, eat it with cheese, on crackers, even stuff hard-cooked (hard-boiled) eggs with it. Makes ½ pound (8 oz/225 g).

⅔ cup (4 oz/100 g) ripe black olives, pitted
⅔ cup (4 oz/100 g) green olives, pitted
10 anchovy fillets, drained
1 tablespoon capers, chopped
1 hard-cooked (hard-boiled) egg yolk
a little fresh thyme
olive oil to moisten

Chop the olives roughly with a knife, then transfer to a mortar. Pound to a paste with a pestle. Pat the anchovy fillets dry with absorbent kitchen paper, then add them to the mortar. Pound until smooth. Add the capers and egg yolk and pound until smooth. Put in the fresh thyme and a trickle of olive oil (the tapenade should not be liquid, just moist enough to spread easily).

Taramasalata made with fresh roes

This is a poor man's taramasalata. The smoked cod's roe traditionally used for this Greek appetizer or dip is deemed a great luxury, but the fresh roes of herring are practically given away. Serves 2-4.

½ pound (8 oz/225 g) fresh herring roes
knob of butter
small piece of garlic
tiny piece of onion
pinch of salt
dash of lemon juice

Lightly fry the roes in butter in a heavy bottomed pan. Then, in a mortar and pestle or a food processor mix in the onion and garlic. Season with salt and lemon.

-BAKES AND-
STEWS

Beef casserole Niçoise

This recipe is based on one of those thick, aromatic Mediterranean dishes which smell almost better than they taste. Ideally it should be made with red wine, but thick tomato sauce with a little red wine vinegar will do. Salt pork belly is better than bacon if you can get it. Don't skip the olives unless you hate them. They give a salty, smoky flavour all their own. Serves 4.

2 pounds beef shank (2 lb/900 g shin of beef)

¼ pound (4 oz/100 g) salt pork belly or bacon

2 tablespoons corn oil

3 onions, roughly chopped

1 16-ounce (14-oz/397-g) can tomatoes

1 tablespoon red wine vinegar

3 cloves garlic, chopped

3 carrots, thinly sliced

1 bouquet garni

½ teaspoon dried rosemary

salt and pepper

10-12 ripe black olives, pitted

tomato paste (purée), (optional)

Cut the beef into thick slices and the pork belly into small strips. Heat the oil in a flameproof casserole. Put the bacon strips in, then add the meat and onions. Turn the meat slices until brown all over. Add the canned tomatoes and wine vinegar, with the garlic, carrots, bouquet garni, rosemary, salt and pepper. Heat together until the stew simmers. Alternatively, the above ingredients may be fried in a skillet (frying pan), then transferred to a casserole.

Transfer the casserole to a moderate oven, 350°F (180°C/Gas Mark 4) and cook for 2½ hours. Add the olives, replace the lid and cook for another 30 minutes. If the casserole seems dry you may add a little tomato paste (purée) diluted with boiling water. Remove the bouquet garni before serving.

Salt cod cooked in milk

Before the days of the deep freezer, salt fish or meats were store cupboard staples for country folk through the long winter season. Serves 4.

1 pound (1 lb/450 g) dried salt cod

2 bay leaves

2-3 tablespoons olive oil

5 large potatoes, peeled and thinly sliced

1 large onion, thinly sliced

1 teaspoon dried oregano

black pepper

1 red or green chili pepper (chilli), de-seeded and finely chopped

5 cups (2 pints/1.1 litres) milk

4 hard-cooked (hard-boiled) eggs, sliced

12 ripe black unstoned olives

a handful of finely chopped parsley

3 cloves garlic, crushed

lemon quarters to serve

Cut the fish into smallish pieces and soak in cold water for 24 hours, renewing the water 2-3 times.

Place the fish in a saucepan with cold water to cover. Add the bay leaves and bring to a simmer, but do not let the water boil or the cod will toughen. Simmer for 5 minutes, then take off the heat and stand for 30 minutes.

Drain the fish, removing the gray skin and bones, and flake coarsely. Cover the base of a wide flameproof earthenware dish with oil, then fill with layers of potatoes, sliced onion and flaked fish, sprinkling oregano and black pepper and chili pepper (chilli) as you go. Pour over milk to just cover, then bake or simmer on top of the stove until the potatoes are tender and the milk has been absorbed.

Decorate the dish with sliced egg and ripe black olives and a sprinkling of parsley and garlic. Lemon quarters can be served alongside.

Bubbling on the Aga in cast-iron pots are Oxtail stew, top left, and Beef casserole Niçoise, bottom right. Meanwhile, Salt cod cooked in milk, top right, and Spicy sausages with polenta, bottom left, keep warm in earthenware dishes.

Spicy sausages with polenta

Polenta is one of those comforting preparations, like mashed potato, which act as complement and blotting paper to highly seasoned or spiced foods, while contributing a soothing texture and taste of their own. The proper peasant version of this dish crumbles Tuscan sausages into a highly flavoured tomato and mushroom sauce; this mixture is then spooned over a thick layer of polenta and served in individual bowls, one for each person. This version is prettier to look at. The polenta is prepared ahead of time. When cool, it is cut into squares and crisped in the oven, then served with the sausages (which can be the best pure meat country sausages around) arranged on top. The sauce is served separately. Serves 4-6.

8-12 good-size all-meat sausages, with herbs or spices

4 tablespoons red wine or water

Polenta:

4 cups (1 ¾ pints/1 litre) salted water

3 cups (1 lb/450 g) fine-grain commeal

¼ stick (1 oz/25 g) butter

1 cup (4 oz/100 g) grated cheese – Parmesan, Pecorino, Cheddar, or a mix

Sauce:

2-3 tablespoons corn or olive oil

1 large onion, chopped

1 carrot, peeled and chopped

1 celery stalk, chopped

2 pounds (2 lb/900 g) juicy tomatoes, or canned equivalent

1 small bunch of parsley, stalks tied

1 fat clove garlic, crushed

¾ ounce (¾ oz/7 g) dried mushrooms, soaked in warm water

½ cup (4 fl oz/125 ml) red wine

salt and pepper

Polenta used for baking needs to be made far enough ahead to cool. Make it the night before or early in the morning. Bring the salted water to a rapid boil in a heavy pot, preferably enamelled cast-iron, then tip the cornmeal in a steady stream into the pot, stirring constantly. After a minute or two it will thicken dramatically. Stirring will become harder, even laborious. Italians claim that they stand stirring for half an hour for perfect polenta, but I find that turning the heat down to a whisper and giving the mixture an occasional vigorous stir with a wooden spoon breaks up any threatening lumps and concentrates the texture. Give it about 40 minutes. Then turn out onto an oiled board, marble slab or large platter. Smooth over and leave to get cold and dense.

To bake the polenta, cut into diamonds or squares. Lay these overlapping one another in an ovenproof dish, dot with the butter and dredge with the grated cheese. Bake at 400°F (200°C/Gas Mark 6) for 30-40 minutes until crisp and golden brown on top.

Meanwhile, the sausages should be cooking at the bottom of the oven. Prick the skins, lay them in a roasting pan, add the little wine or water, loosely cover with foil and bake for 30 minutes, turning now and then.

While the sausages are cooking, prepare the sauce. Heat the oil in a pan and soften the onion, carrot and celery. Add the tomatoes, parsley and garlic. Drain the mushrooms, adding their soaking water to the pan. Chop the mushrooms and add them too. Bring to a fairly fast boil and cook covered until the vegetables soften. Add the red wine, reduce the heat and simmer until thickened and tasty. Add salt and pepper to taste. For the last 10 minutes, if you wish, the sausages can be combined with the sauce to allow flavours to blend, or the sauce can be served separately.

Below: Stuffed pumpkin, served in a hand-potted stoneware dish. Use a generous ladle to scoop out servings of stuffing and pumpkin onto individual plates.

Oxtail stew

Oxtail makes a rich, thick stew with a good meaty flavour. The pieces of tail should be washed, dipped in boiling water and dried before being fried with the onions. Plainly cooked, home-grown vegetables such as boiled potatoes, carrots or cabbage go best with oxtail. Serves 4.

1 medium-size oxtail, jointed

1 tablespoon all-purpose (plain) flour

salt and pepper

¼ stick (1 oz/25 g) butter

2 onions, sliced

2 carrots, scraped and sliced

1 stalk celery, sliced

1 turnip, peeled and sliced

2 cloves

pinch of mace

juice of ½ lemon

Separate the jointed pieces of oxtail. Wash them, dip them in boiling water for 1 minute, then dry them carefully. Roll the pieces in flour seasoned with salt and pepper.

Melt the butter in a heavy flameproof casserole. When it sizzles, put in the pieces of meat and sliced onions. Turn them over so that the meat browns on all sides. Add the carrots, celery and turnip, with the spices. Pour over enough water to cover the lot. Bring the liquid to a boil, skimming off any scum which rises in the pan. Reduce the temperature to simmering point, cover the pot with a piece of foil or waxed (greaseproof) paper and the lid. Simmer very slowly for 3 hours or longer, if you are not in a hurry. The meat should be falling off the bone.

Taste the stock and add salt and pepper if needed. Should you feel up to it, the appearance of the dish will be improved if you pick out the pieces of meat and put the stock and vegetables through a sieve, returning the thickened stock and meat to the pot for a few minutes to heat up again. Either way add the lemon juice just before serving.

Stuffed pumpkin

Nowadays, markets sell not only pumpkin in season, but also many of its more arcane relations. Any good dense squash can be stuffed in the same way, but you may need to adjust the quantity of stuffing. The quantity below will serve 6.

1 pumpkin

1 generous tablespoon soft light brown sugar

½ stick (2 oz/50 g) butter

1 tablespoon oil

2 onions, finely chopped

1 clove garlic, crushed

1 cup ground lamb or beef (8 oz/225 g minced lamb or beef)

½ cup pignoli (2 oz/50 g pine nuts)

½ cup (2 oz/50 g) slivered almonds

⅓ cup (2 oz/50 g) dried or fresh dates, chopped

1 teaspoon cinnamon

2 cups (8 oz/225 g) cooked rice

salt and pepper

Cut the stalk end off the pumpkin to use as a lid. Scoop out the seeds and the fibre, then spread the brown sugar around the inside with a wooden spoon. Melt the butter in the oil in a large skillet (frying pan) and brown the onions. Add the garlic, then the ground (minced) meat, turning it until it is brown all over.

In a second small pan lightly toast the pignoli (pine nuts) and almonds (use no oil but keep moving the pan to prevent the nuts from scorching). Add the nuts, dates, cinnamon and rice to the meat. Season with salt and plenty of pepper.

Fill the pumpkin with the meat mixture. Fit the stalk end back on top and put the pumpkin on a baking sheet. Bake at 375°F (190°C/Gas Mark 5) for at least 1 hour or until the pumpkin is soft.

Fried chicken and potatoes in walnut sauce

This recipe can be provisioned from a kitchen garden, possibly even down to the chicken. If not, you may be lucky enough to have – as I do – an excellent local supermarket with fresh supplies of cilantro (coriander). Substituting toasted almonds for the walnuts and cilantro for the herbs listed above right gives a deliciously different sauce. Serves 4.

1½ cups (6 oz/175 g) fresh young walnuts

5 cloves garlic

a handful of fresh large-leafed parsley

a handful of fresh basil

salt

about ⅔ cup (¼ pint/150 ml) olive oil

2 tablespoons butter

1 or 2 sprigs of rosemary

3 pound (3 lb/1.4 kg) chicken, cut into serving pieces or 4 chicken thighs

2 pounds (2 lb/900 g) potatoes, peeled and quartered

Shell and peel the walnuts and chop them finely (or crush in a mortar and pestle) with the cloves of garlic, parsley and basil. Add salt to taste and stir in about ½ cup (4 fl oz/125 ml) of the olive oil until a dense sauce is formed.

Melt the butter in the remaining oil. Add the rosemary and the chicken pieces and sauté until browned on all sides. Using a slotted spoon, remove the chicken pieces from the pan. Put the quartered potatoes into the hot oil and sauté until they are brown all over. Then return the chicken to the pan (discard the rosemary which will have done its work) and allow them to cook together over a gentle heat for about 30 minutes until the potatoes are ready.

Remove the chicken and potatoes from the oily pan to a warmed earthenware dish and tip over the walnut sauce. Turn the chicken and potatoes until they are coated in the sauce and serve immediately.

Below: Chick peas Catalan, baked in a hand-made stoneware pot. Cooking this dish in an Aga has given it a crispy top.

Pork and beans

Also known as Boston Baked Beans, this recipe is a classic of American domestic cookery and the inspiration of the ubiquitous canned baked beans. The Puritan settlers prepared this dish in bulk on a Saturday night, baking it slowly in an earthenware pot. They ate some for supper that night and observed the Sabbath by serving the rest for Sunday meals. Traditionally, this filling dish is accompanied by chunks of hearty home-made brown bread which is used to soak up the sauce. Serves 4.

2 cups (1 lb/450 g) dried haricot (navy) beans soaked overnight in water

2 tablespoons molasses (black treacle)

a dash of Worcestershire Sauce

2½ teaspoons mustard powder

2½ teaspoons soft light brown sugar

salt

pepper

½ pound (8 oz/225 g) streaky pork (salt or otherwise), derinded and cut into chunks

1 large onion, sliced

Cook the navy (haricot) beans for 1½-2 hours in the water they were soaked in. Strain the beans, reserving the water in a clean pan. Put the beans in a casserole and set aside.

Heat the bean water and stir into it the molasses (treacle), Worcestershire Sauce, mustard, sugar, salt and pepper. Add the pork and onion to the beans, then pour over the flavoured bean water. If necessary, add hot water to come just over the top of the beans.

Cover and bake at 350°F (180°C/Gas Mark 4) for about 1 hour or until the beans are soft. During this time, if the beans seem to be getting too dry, add more hot water.

Chick peas Catalan

Chick peas have a nutty flavour quite unlike any other dried vegetable. The Spanish make great use of them in stews and casseroles, together with *chorizos* (highly spiced sausages), odd bits of meat or game, herbs, wine and lots of garlic. This adaptation of a Catalan dish serves 4 people. Some delicatessen stock *chorizos*, but any highly spiced Continental-style boiling sausage could be substituted.

2 cups (1 lb/450 g) chick peas, soaked in water for 24 hours, rinsed and drained
1 large onion, roughly chopped
1 carrot, scraped and sliced
1 stalk celery, sliced
1 ham (bacon) bone with trimmings
1 bouquet garni
3 tablespoons olive oil
1 chorizo or other spiced sausage
2½ cups (1 pt/600 ml) homemade tomato sauce or 1 x 5 oz
(142 g) can tomato paste (purée)
1 clove garlic, crushed
2 tablespoons chopped parsley
salt and pepper

Put the chick peas in plenty of fresh water in a large pan with the onion, carrot and celery. Push the ham (bacon) bone down among the chick peas, together with the bouquet garni. Add 2 tablespoons of the oil to the cooking water.

Bring the contents of the pan slowly to a boil, skimming if necessary, and boil steadily over lowest heat for 2 hours or until the chick peas are tender. Add the sausage and cook for a further 2-3 hours.

Strain the stock into a bowl, remove the bouquet garni and transfer the chick peas, vegetables and ham (bacon) to a flameproof casserole.

If you are using tomato sauce, dilute it with enough of the cooking liquid to cover the peas. If you are using tomato paste (purée), mix the contents of the can with the stock. Pour the liquid over the peas, mixing well. Continue cooking, covered, on top of the stove over a low heat for another 1-2 hours. Alternatively, bake the dish, covered, at 325°F (160°C/Gas Mark 3) for about the same length of time. If the dish seems to be getting too dry, add any remaining stock from the peas or a little boiling water. About 15 minutes before serving, stir in the garlic, parsley and remaining olive oil. Add salt and pepper to taste. Remove the bouquet garni.

Serve with the sausage cut into chunks and the ham (bacon) removed from the bone. Thick rounds of French bread moistened with a little olive oil, salt and crushed garlic would be appropriate with this dish.

Rabbit with prunes

When the harvest has been gathered in, it is time for a celebration meal for 6. Rabbits, freely available at this time of year, get the luxury treatment with prunes and wine.

2 rabbits
½ cup (4 fl oz/125 ml) olive oil
1½ cups (12 fl oz/350 ml) red wine
1½ cups (12 fl oz/350 ml) dry marsala
1 teaspoon fresh or dried marjoram or thyme
1 cup (6 fl oz/175 g) dried prunes
6 cloves garlic, crushed
ground black pepper

Joint the rabbits, cutting each saddle into 2 pieces. Marinate meat in 6 tablespoons of the olive oil, the red wine, half the marsala, the thyme and prunes until the prunes are soft. Drain, reserving marinade and prunes.

Heat the remaining olive oil in a large cast-iron casserole and sauté the garlic and rabbit until the rabbit is browned all over.

Pour over the rest of the marsala and turn the rabbit over in it until it has reduced by two-thirds. Pour over the reserved marinade with the prunes. Season with salt, cover, reduce the heat and simmer very gently for 1½-2 hours until the rabbit is very tender. Take the lid off toward the end, if necessary, to reduce the liquid to a rich but plentiful sauce. Pepper it very generously. Serve with egg *pappardelle* or noodles.

Right: Rabbit with prunes, baked and served in hand-potted stoneware. The flavour of the meat is brought out by marinating it before cooking (above).

—RICE AND—
PASTA

Spaghetti with lemon

This tangy and summery pasta sauce can be made more substantial by adding pieces of cooked chicken tossed in butter and chives. For the best flavour, use the richer and more expensive spaghetti *all' uovo* (made with egg). Serves 3-4.

salt
grated rind and juice of 1 large lemon
¾ cup (6 fl oz/175 ml) fresh cream or crème fraiche
1 teaspoon grated nutmeg
1 teaspoon ground black pepper
4 cups (1 lb/450 g) spaghetti
freshly grated Parmesan cheese to serve

Fill a large pan with lightly salted water and bring it to a boil. Put the lemon rind and juice into the dish in which the spaghetti is to be served. Add the cream or *crème fraiche*, the nutmeg and the pepper.

Cook the spaghetti until it is *al dente*, drain, and toss in the lemon mixture. Serve with plenty of freshly grated Parmesan.

Orecchiette with peas and mint

A wonderful way to use the first peas from the garden. The same recipe works beautifully if baby zucchini (courgettes) are substituted for the peas, but there is no need to blanch them. Serves 4.

salt
2 pounds (2 lb/900 g) fresh new peas, hulled
1 stick (4 oz/100 g) butter
2 shallots, finely chopped
4 cups (1 lb/450 g) orecchiette
a bunch of fresh mint, torn-up

Fill a large saucepan with plenty of salted water for the pasta and put it on a high heat. Blanch the peas briefly in a small saucepan of boiling water. Strain the peas but keep the water in which they were blanched.

Melt the butter in a heavy pan and sauté the chopped shallots; do not let them brown. Start cooking the *orecchiette* in the boiling water.

When the pasta is almost done, make the sauce by adding the peas to the soft shallots and cooking over low heat, adding the mint leaves, salt and 1-2 tablespoons of the pea liquor. Drain the pasta and pile it in a warmed serving dish, with the sauce on top.

Fettucine with broccoli and anchovy

This recipe seems almost too primitive to be interesting, so simple is its method: chopped broccoli is heated through with anchovies melted into a *salsa verde* mixture of herbs and garlic, the whole lot stirred into a heap of fine noodles. Quick, satisfying and delicious, it is an excellent way to make one or two bundles of broccoli feed 4 or so people in style. You could serve a salad beforehand, but the pasta should be eaten solo.

1 pound (1 lb/450 g) broccoli
salt and plenty of freshly ground black pepper
4 cups (1 lb/450 g) freshly-made fettucine
6 tablespoons extra-virgin olive oil
8 canned anchovy fillets plus some of the oil from the can
4-6 cloves garlic, finely chopped
a generous handful of parsley and/or basil, finely chopped

It is best to cook the broccoli stems ahead of the florets, otherwise by the time the stems are *al dente* the tops will be a mush. Cut off the stems just below the heads, and throw into a pan of salted boiling water. After 3 minutes add the florets, and cook for another 2-3 minutes. Alternatively, put the florets in a steamer on top of the same pan. The broccoli should remain just crisp and green, as it will get more cooking during the final assembly stage. Drain.

Meanwhile, drop the *fettucine* into a large pan of boiling salted water, stirring briefly to loosen. Turn the heat down slightly and cook for 2-3 minutes until *al dente*. Drain and refresh under cold running water. Drain thoroughly again.

When cold, cut the broccoli into smallish pieces – not a mush nor big chunks, but somewhere in between. Set aside.

In a large earthenware dish on a flame tamer (wire mat), first heat the olive oil, then add the chopped anchovy fillets and a little of their oil. When the anchovies disintegrate, add the chopped garlic and herbs. Heat for 1 minute over gentle heat, stirring well to prevent the garlic from burning. Add the broccoli, forking it around in the anchovy mixture until hot. Finally, add the fettucine, forking it around briskly to coat and loosen.

Right: Fettucine with broccoli and anchovy, served on hand-painted Mediterranean pottery.

Date and mussel risotto

If you haven't the time for stirring risotto this makes a very good sauce for pasta – choose a shape which echoes the mussels or something marine like shells. Arborio rice is traditionally used, although American long-grain rice makes a tasty, if less than authentic risotto. Serves 4.

24 mussels, scrubbed and debearded

½ bottle white wine

4 tablespoons butter

2 tablespoons oil

3 cloves garlic, crushed

2 leeks, sliced

2 cups (14 oz/400 g) arborio rice

½ teaspoon powdered saffron, or to taste

⅔ cup (4 oz/100 g) fresh or preserved dates, pitted and halved

salt, pepper and brown sugar to taste

Put the mussels into a heavy saucepan over a moderate heat and throw in the white wine. Put a lid on and "sweat" the mussels for 5-8 minutes until they open. Using a slotted spoon, transfer the mussels to a bowl. Discard any that have failed to open. Set the mussel liquid aside.

Melt 2 tablespoons of the butter in the oil in a wide sauté pan and heat the garlic and leeks for 1-2 minutes. Put in the rice. When the rice turns translucent start to tip in some of the reserved liquid from the mussels. When the juice is finished continue with water until the rice is almost ready. Now add the saffron, dissolved in a little boiling water. Meanwhile, discard at least some of the mussel shells, although it's pretty to keep some in the dish.

In a second pan melt the remaining butter and add the dates. Add the slimmed-down heap of mussels. (You can melt a teaspoon of brown sugar in at this point if you are using fresh dates and would like the dish exotically sweet; preserved dates will be sweet enough.) When the dates are warmed through and buttery, stir them into the risotto. Add water cautiously until the rice is cooked – though still with a bite. Taste and season with plenty of black pepper, then serve at once.

Greek roast lamb with pasta

Highly spiced and coloured, this is a festive supper dish which persuades a leg of lamb to feed up to 8 people.

1 leg of lamb, about 5 pounds (5 lb/2.25 kg)

1 tablespoon ground cumin

1 tablespoon ground coriander

1 bulb garlic (reserve 1 clove and cut the rest into slivers)

2-3 sprigs fresh oregano

½ cup (4 fl oz/125 ml) white wine, preferably Retsina

3 tablespoons extra-virgin olive oil

2-3 dried red chili peppers (chillies)

4 or 5 peeled plum tomatoes, chopped

squeeze of tomato paste (purée)

4 cups (1 lb/450 g) chunky pasta shapes

Stab the lamb in several places with a sharp blade, rub it all over with the ground cumin and coriander, then fill the slits with slivers of bruised garlic and oregano leaves. Put the lamb into a shallow bowl, pour over the wine and olive oil and leave to marinate for 2-3 hours or longer. Drain the lamb, reserving the marinade, and transfer it to a roasting pan.

Roast the lamb at 350°F (180°C/Gas Mark 4), giving it 20-25 minutes per lb (450 g), adding a bit more time if you don't like it pink. Baste it with its fat. Three-quarters of the way through the cooking time, pour the fat off into a wide sauté or paella-type pan and set aside. Continue basting the lamb, using the reserved marinade.

Crush the remaining clove of garlic and add it to the lamb fat in the pan with the dried red chili peppers (chillies), the tomatoes and the tomato paste (purée). Crush the mixture over the heat with a wooden spoon.

Put the pasta into a large pan of boiling salted water as you take the lamb from the oven. Remove the lamb to a board to rest but place the roasting pan with its juices over a low heat. When the pasta is *al dente*, drain, tip it into the roasting pan and turn it in the pan juices until coated in the savoury brown glaze. Stir the hot pasta into the sauce in the sauté pan and place the lamb on top, carved into rough hunks.

Left: Date & mussel risotto, cooked in a stainless steel skillet (frying pan) and served on a brightly painted Italian plate. If you wish, grate a sprinkle of Parmesan over each serving.

-TARTS AND-
PIES

Potato pie

A filling and comforting pie that consists of a yeast crust packed around alternate layers of sliced potato and a savoury pork and spinach mixture. Serve hot, or pack for a picnic with a crisp salad of mixed leaves. Serves 12.

Yeast dough:

¼ teaspoon sugar

1¼ cups (½ pint/300 ml) tepid water

1 package active dry yeast (¼ oz/7 g dried yeast)

4 cups all-purpose flour (1 lb/450 g plain flour)

pinch of salt

¾ stick (3 oz/75 g) butter, softened

1 egg

Filling:

1 pound ground pork (1 lb/450 g minced pork)

a handful of spinach, sorrel or chard, finely chopped

a handful of parsley, finely chopped

2-3 cloves garlic, crushed

3 shallots or a small bunch of scallions (spring onions), finely chopped

salt and pepper

a sprinkling of ground mace or grated nutmeg

6 cups sliced potatoes (2 lb/900 g) potatoes, peeled and finely sliced

Left: Potato pie, cooked in a simple white baking dish. The yeast crust tops a filling made from alternate layers of potato and pork and spinach mixture.

Dissolve the sugar in half the tepid water. Add the yeast, stir and leave for 10 minutes until frothy. Warm the flour and salt slightly in a large bowl. Rub in the butter. Make a well in the flour, then stir in the yeast liquid with the beaten egg, adding enough of the remaining water to make a soft dough. Knead until smooth and elastic then return the dough to a clean bowl, cover and leave to rise in a warm place for 2 hours.

Preheat the oven to 425°F (220°C/Gas Mark 7). Make the pie filling. Mix the ground (minced) pork with the spinach, sorrel or chard. Add the parsley, garlic, shallots or scallions (spring onions) and seasonings.

On a floured board, roll out three-quarters of the dough thinly and line a 12-inch (30-cm) pie dish, bringing the dough up the sides and leaving a lip all around. Fill the pie with alternate layers of potato slices and pork mixture, finishing with the pork. Roll out the remaining dough to a round that will fit the top of the pie. Fit it in place, and damp and seal the edges. Cut a hole in the middle of the crust for steam to escape.

Bake the pie for 20 minutes to get the yeast dough off to a good start, then lower the temperature to 350°F (180°C/Gas Mark 4) and bake for 1 hour more, capping the pie with foil toward the end of this time, to prevent the crust from overbrowning.

Pigeon pie

The sort of rich and hearty traditional country dish which is coming back into favour. Serves 4-6.

2 pigeons

4 bacon slices, rindless

1 large onion, chopped

2-3 tablespoons butter

½ pound hind shank or neck (8 oz/225 g stewing steak), trimmed of fat and cubed

1 tablespoon all-purpose (plain) flour

salt and pepper

1¼ cups dark beer (½ pint/300 ml stout)

2 tablespoons wine vinegar

pinch of dried thyme

1 bay leaf

Rich pie dough (rich shortcrust pastry):

1½ cups all-purpose flour (6 oz/175 g plain flour)

½ teaspoon salt

7 tablespoons butter

1 egg yolk

1-2 tablespoons cold water

1 egg, beaten, to glaze

milk

Make the pie dough (shortcrust pastry) by sifting the flour and salt into a bowl and rubbing in the butter. Beat the egg yolk and water together and stir into the flour mixture to make a firm dough. Wrap in waxed (greaseproof) paper and leave to stand in a cool place for at least 1 hour.

Have the pigeons split in half. Wrap each half in a slice of bacon. Sauté the onion lightly in the butter until transparent. Add the beef cubes, frying until lightly browned all over.

Sprinkle on the flour with a pinch each of salt and black pepper, and stir for 1-2 minutes. Pour on beer and vinegar, with the pinch of thyme and bay leaf.

Bring to a boil, lower the heat and simmer for 10-15 minutes or until the sauce has thickened.

Cover the base of a large pie dish or roasting pan with half the meat/onion mixture. Lay the pigeon halves on top and cover with the remainder of the meat and juices. With a sheet of foil, cover the dish carefully, pressing the foil down around the edges, and cook in a cool oven at 275°F (140°C/Gas Mark 1) for 2½ hours. Then, take out of the oven, remove the foil and leave to cool, skimming off as much fat as possible. Raise the oven temperature to 425°F (220°C/Gas Mark 7).

Roll out the dough on a floured board, to a round ¼ inch (5 mm) thick, and slightly larger than the size of the pie dish. Stand an inverted egg cup in the middle of the dish to support the piecrust. Cut a long strip of dough from the scraps and stick this around the moistened rim of the pie dish. Moisten with milk and lay the piecrust on top, crimping the edges with a fork. Decorate with leaf-shaped dough cut-outs, prick a few holes with a skewer and glaze with beaten egg.

Return the dish to the hot oven and bake for 20 minutes, or until the piecrust is golden, then reduce the heat to 375°F (190°C/Gas Mark 5) and bake for 20-30 minutes more.

Spiced apple and walnut pie

A sweet batter pudding that can be served hot for dessert or cold for a snack, this is an easy pie for those times when you've got too many apples. It is particularly splendid made with fresh walnuts if you're lucky enough to have a tree. Serves 4-6.

5 biggish cooking or firm eating apples

juice of 1 lemon

10 tablespoons self-rising flour

(65 g/2½ oz self-raising flour)

pinch of salt

1 teaspoon ground cinnamon (more if you like)

⅓ cup superfine sugar (75 g/3 oz caster sugar)

½ cup (4 fl oz/125 ml) milk

1 drop of vanilla essence

2 eggs

4 tablespoons corn oil

sugar for dusting

½ stick (2 oz/50 g) butter

½ cup (2 oz/50 g) broken walnuts

Peel the apples. Slice them into a bowl and pour lemon juice over them to stop them browning. Grease a medium-sized flan dish or cake pan. Preheat the oven to 400-425°F (200-220°C/Gas Mark 6-7).

Make a batter with the flour, salt, cinnamon, sugar, milk, vanilla essence, eggs and oil – this can be done very quickly in a food processor or blender. Alternatively, mix the dry ingredients in a bowl, make a well in the middle and add the liquids. Beat well, gradually incorporating the flour until a smooth batter is formed. Pour it into the flan dish. Arrange the slices of apple on top of the batter – in a haphazard way or with patisserie smartness, as you like.

Scatter a little more sugar, small lumps of butter and the broken nuts all over the flan and bake it for 45 minutes-1 hour, until puffed up and golden in colour.

Cherry tart

One of the most beautiful-looking open fruit tarts. Make it when cherries are at their ripest and cheapest, using the dark, sweet kind. At other times you could use canned cherries. In either case, the stones should be removed. This is a slightly tedious job, but it greatly improves the tart. Serves 6.

2-2½ pounds (2-2½ lb/900-1.1 kg) dark cherries, pitted
½ cup (4 oz/100 g) sugar
3 tablespoons redcurrant jelly
1 tablespoon water

Pie dough (shortcrust pastry):
1 cup all-purpose flour (4 oz/100 g plain flour) plus extra for rolling
¼ teaspoon salt
¼ cup (2 oz/50 g) margarine

Make the pie dough (shortcrust pastry) by sifting the flour and salt into a bowl and rubbing in the fat. Add enough cold water to make a stiff dough.

Roll out the dough on a floured surface and line an 8-inch (20-cm) flan ring set on a baking sheet.

Arrange the pitted cherries close together on the dough. Sprinkle with the sugar. Bake for 30-40 minutes at 400°F (200°C/Gas Mark 6).

When the tart has cooled a little, melt the redcurrant jelly in a pan with the water, and pour over the top of the cherries to glaze them attractively.

Left: Cherry tart, right, in its baking pan, and Spiced apple and walnut pie, far right, served in a stoneware baking dish.

SALADS

Tuscan bread and tomato salad

European peasant cookery is full of ideas for recycling the fine, dense bread, crumby and a touch sour, whose only fault is its tendency to dry out overnight. Although this Tuscan salad made with stale bread and tomatoes is of rock-bottom simplicity, this does not prevent it appearing on menus of smart restaurants specializing in rustic food. Not to be contemplated for stale sliced supermarket loaves, but excellent for using up hard stubs of homemade bread. Eat as an appetizer, or with something light like an omelette, sliced salami or prosciutto, or soused or broiled (grilled) fish. Serves 4.

6 or more chunks of hard, stale bread

6 ripe, juicy tomatoes, peeled and roughly chopped

1 large onion, or 1 bunch of scallions (spring onions), peeled and chopped quite small, but with some green left on

½ cucumber, part-peeled and diced

1 large sprig of basil and/or parsley, finely chopped

1 clove garlic, crushed

3 tablespoons fruity olive oil

salt and pepper

2 tablespoons red wine vinegar

Soak the bread in cold water for 15 minutes. Squeeze out as much water as possible, then crumble into a large bowl. Add the chopped vegetables, herbs, garlic, olive oil, salt and pepper and fork through to mix.

Chill the salad in the refrigerator or pantry for 1-2 hours, adding vinegar to taste and a sprinkle more herbs just before serving.

Green beans Provençale

Ideally use snap beans or haricots verts (French beans), but snake (runner) beans can be substituted at the start of the season, when they are reasonably small and tender. The anchovies give a subtle but not fishy flavour. Beans cooked like this are good cold, in which case use olive oil instead of butter and squeeze lemon juice over them. Serves 4.

1 pound snap beans or haricots verts (1 lb/450 g French beans), trimmed

salt

1 tablespoon butter

1 clove garlic, peeled but left whole

2 anchovies, pounded until smooth

Put the beans into a pan of boiling salted water and cook until tender – about 8-10 minutes. Drain.

Melt the butter with the garlic in a pan over gentle heat. Add the beans and stir until they have absorbed the butter. Stir in the anchovies and heat through. Remove garlic before serving.

Dandelion salad with hot bacon dressing

Young tender dandelion leaves make a tasty salad, either mixed with other greens or on their own. If the dandelions are growing in your garden, you can make them more tender by laying a tile over the plant. With wild ones just take the youngest leaves as they are less bitter.

dandelion leaves

assortment of salad greens

3-4 bacon slices, cut in squares

1 tablespoon red wine vinegar

Wash and dry the dandelion leaves and other greens and set aside, whole, in a serving dish. To make the dressing, put the bacon squares into a pan over a moderate heat, until the fat has melted a bit and the bacon is crisp. Quickly stir the vinegar into the fat, and pour the whole lot over the salad. Serve at once.

Warm pepper salad

Now that peppers, in their gorgeous motley of green, scarlet and gold, are available all year around, you can make this salad as often as you like. Dress it copiously, and let it stand for five minutes before serving with crusty bread to mop up the delicious juices. When I first ate this as an appetizer, just before Christmas, it was made entirely with festive red peppers that vied with the holly berries.

1 large pepper per person

4 tablespoons olive oil

2 anchovy fillets per pepper

2-3 fat cloves garlic, crushed

1-2 tablespoons capers, drained and chopped

salt and pepper

Broil (grill) the peppers. The easiest way to do this, I find, is to sit them on a gas ring, one at a time, turning them as they blacken. More elegant is to skewer them on a fork and turn them in the flame, which can also be a wood fire or barbecue. If these methods are not possible, cut the peppers in half and layer them in a broiler (grill) pan lined with foil. Grill them until the skin chars and becomes flaky. Then remove the black outer skin, leaving the partially cooked pepper with a sweet intensity of flavour and a limp, juicy texture.

As each pepper cooks, transfer it to a plastic bag to steam gently (this makes the skin easier to remove) while you prepare the lusty Sicilian dressing.

Heat the olive oil gently in a small pan and mash in the anchovies, stirring until they dissolve into the oil. Add the crushed garlic and capers with salt and pepper to taste. Stir briefly then remove but keep warm.

Next, take a pepper, and with a blunt knife scrape off as much charred outer skin as you can. Halve the pepper and remove the seeds, membranes, and stalk. To loosen any last clinging black shreds, run the pepper under a cold faucet (tap), or dip into cold water, and use your fingernails. A little charred skin left behind will not wreck the flavour, but it will mar the look of the dish. As each pepper is dealt with, cut it lengthwise into thick strips and lay these in a dish with the dressing, turning to coat them. Repeat this process until you have filled the dish – a flat, oval or round pottery dish is becoming – and then serve.

*Top: West Coast salad, served on a
generous pottery plate. Bottom: Warm
pepper salad (below right) and Bean
and cucumber salad, served on hand-
painted Mediterranean dishes.*

*Top: Tuscan bread and tomato salad
(right) and Green beans Provençale
(left), served on Provençal pottery.
Bottom: Dandelion salad with hot
bacon dressing, in an antique dish.*

Smoked mackerel salad with radicchio and hot potatoes

I always love a hot potato salad, and this one which Richard Stein includes in his *English Seafood Cookery* is a favourite. He uses dandelion leaves instead of radicchio, but these are hard to get in town. I love these colours, the dark red leaf with the pale orange of the mackerel. Red or bronze-leafed lettuce may be used in place of radicchio, and smoked tuna may be substituted for mackerel. Serves 4.

1 smoked mackerel

1 pound (1 lb/450 g) new potatoes

1 onion, finely chopped

1 small radicchio or oakleaf lettuce, torn into manageable pieces

Dressing:

6 tablespoons olive or hazelnut oil

2 tablespoons white wine vinegar

¼ teaspoon mustard powder

salt and pepper

Take the bones and the skin from the mackerel and cut into even slices. Scrub the potatoes and boil them for 15-20 minutes or until tender – there should be no need to peel them. Make the dressing by shaking all the ingredients together in a screw-top jar.

When the potatoes are ready, cut them up roughly and put them back in their warm pan – turn the heat up high and very quickly throw in the onion, the radicchio or oakleaf lettuce and the dressing. After just a few seconds put the salad into a bowl, throw on the mackerel pieces and serve immediately.

Bean and cucumber salad

Very new and small fava (broad) beans are tender and good eaten lightly blanched as a salad. The quantities below will serve 2-4.

1 pound fava beans (1 lb/450 g broad beans), hulled

2 teaspoons chopped fresh herbs

1 cucumber, finely diced

Dressing:

1 egg, hard-cooked (hard-boiled)

2-3 tablespoons light (single) cream

Bring a pan of water to a boil, add the beans and cook for 1 minute. Drain, refresh under cold running water and drain again.

Mix the beans, herbs and cucumber in a bowl. To make the dressing, pound the hard-cooked (hard-boiled) egg yolk and mix with the chopped egg white. Moisten with the cream.

Pour the dressing over the salad. A few shrimps may be added to turn this simple salad into a light meal.

West Coast salad

A salad of the freshest local ingredients from sunny California, cooked up by chef Richard Irving of The Ivy Restaurant, Los Angeles. Serves 4.

2 corn cobs

1 pound zucchini (1 lb/450 g courgettes)

1 pound (1 lb/450 g) mushrooms

1 bunch scallions (spring onions)

1 pound (1 lb/450 g) shrimp in shells (prawns)

1 head radicchio, shredded

1 head oakleaf lettuce, shredded

1 cucumber, roughly chopped

2 avocados, peeled and chopped

4 tomatoes, peeled and chopped

Vinaigrette:

2 tablespoons olive oil

1 tablespoon red wine vinegar

1 teaspoon ground chili powder

To serve:

1 lime

1 lemon

Barbecue or charcoal grill the whole corn, zucchini (courgettes), mushrooms, scallions (spring onions) and shrimps (prawns). Meanwhile, mix the radicchio, lettuce, cucumber, avocado and tomato together and toss them in the spicy vinaigrette. Strip the grilled corn from its cob and add it to the cold ingredients, along with the other grilled vegetables, chopped, and the prawns. Serve with wedges of lime and lemon.

Smoked mackerel salad with radicchio and hot potatoes, served on Scottish tartanware.

BREADS

Barm brack

This delicious sweet bread is a traditional Celtic recipe.

2 tablespoons soft light brown sugar

1 ¼ cups (½ pt/300 ml) lukewarm milk

1 package active dry yeast (¼ oz/7 g dried yeast)

4 cups all-purpose or bread flour

(1 lb/450 g strong plain flour)

⅔ cup golden raisins (4 oz/100 g sultanas)

½ cup (3 oz/75 g) dried currants

2 tablespoons candied peel

½ stick (2 oz/50 g) butter or margarine

a pinch of allspice

a pinch of salt

1 egg, beaten

1 tablespoon clear honey to glaze

Dissolve 1 teaspoon of the sugar in half the milk. Add the yeast, stir and leave for 10 minutes until frothy. Warm the flour slightly in one bowl and the dried fruit and peel in another. Rub the fat into the flour, then stir in the fruit, peel, spice, remaining sugar and salt and mix well.

Make a well in the flour, add the yeast mixture and the egg, then as much of the remaining warm milk as is needed to make a soft dough. Knead until smooth and elastic, then return the dough to the clean bowl, cover and leave to rise in a warm place for 2 hours.

Turn out the risen dough onto a floured board and knead for 5 minutes. Put into a greased, warmed 7-cup (3-pint/1.75-litre) loaf pan and place in an oiled polythene bag to rise for 30 minutes.

Bake at 400°F (200°C/Gas Mark 6) for 10 minutes. Lower heat to 325°F (160°C/Gas Mark 3) and cook for a further 30-45 minutes, or until the bread is firm and has shrunk away slightly from the sides of the pan. Turn out bread onto a cooling rack and brush the top with the honey to glaze. Eat cold.

Buttermilk biscuits (scones)

Buttermilk makes these teatime treats light and tasty. If buttermilk is not available, you should substitute sour milk (thickened but not separated). The quantities given below will make about 12 good-sized biscuits (scones). You can use wholemeal flour, instead of all-purpose, if you wish.

2 cups all-purpose flour (8 oz/225 g plain flour)

1 teaspoon baking powder

pinch of salt

¼ stick (1 oz/25 g) butter or margarine

¼ teaspoon baking soda (bicarbonate of soda)

⅔ cup (¼ pint/150 ml) buttermilk

Preheat the oven to 400°F (200°C/Gas Mark 6). Sift the flour, baking powder and salt into a bowl. Rub in the butter until the mixture resembles fine crumbs. Dissolve the baking soda in the buttermilk and stir into the dry ingredients until the dough is smooth and leaves the bowl's sides clean.

On a floured board, roll the dough out to a thickness of about ¾ inch (2 cm). Stamp out into rounds about the diameter of a coffee cup. Lay these on a greased baking sheet.

Bake for 10 minutes then reduce the oven temperature to 350°F (180°C/Gas Mark 4) and cook for another 5-10 minutes, or until the biscuits (scones) are golden.

Soda bread

The traditional Irish bread, made without yeast. It is a useful standby for times when bread supplies run out. A handful of currants or golden raisins (sultanas) added to the dough make the basic mix into a nice tea bread which can be eaten hot from the oven, with butter. Ideally the bread should be made with buttermilk, but ordinary milk which has gone sour (thickened but not separated) may be substituted.

4 cups all-purpose flour (1 lb/450 g plain flour)

1 teaspoon salt

1 teaspoon baking soda (bicarbonate of soda)

1 teaspoon sugar (optional)

buttermilk (see method)

Sift the dry ingredients into a large bowl. Make a well in the middle and gradually add the buttermilk, little by little, stirring in the flour at the same time, until you have a soft dough and the bowl is fairly clean. Preheat the oven to 425°F (220°C/Gas Mark 6).

Turn the dough onto a floured board and knead lightly then pat out into a round about 1¼ inches (3.5 cm) thick.

Lay the dough round on a lightly greased baking sheet and, using a sharp knife, make a cross-shaped cut in the middle. Bake for about 35 minutes. Remove the bread from the baking sheet and tap the bottom to make sure it is cooked through – it should sound hollow. Set it to cool or eat warm.

Left: Soda bread, middle, Barm brack, top, and Buttermilk biscuits (scones), made with wholemeal flour, bottom.

Far left: Soda bread and Buttermilk biscuits (scones) with Gooseberry and Dried apricot jams and Lemon curd (for preserve recipes see p. 165).

Cottage loaf

A cottage loaf brings the look of a country kitchen to your table.

2 teaspoons active dry (dried) yeast

1 teaspoon sugar or honey

1 1/4-1 3/4 cups (10-14 fl oz/300-400 ml) warm water

6 cups all-purpose (1 1/2 lb/675 g plain or bread) flour

2 teaspoons salt

oil (see method)

Dissolve the yeast and sugar or honey in 1/4 cup (60 ml/ 2 fl oz) of the warm water and set the mixture aside until it foams. Sift the flour with the salt into a warmed bowl then tip onto a floured working surface. Make a well in the middle and tip in the yeast mixture. Use your hands to draw the flour into the liquid. Keep adding warm water a splash at a time until the liquid binds the flour. Knead the dough for 10-20 minutes.

Put the dough in a mixing bowl, smear a drop of oil over it to stop a crust forming and put a clean cloth over the bowl. Choose a raising time which suits your schedule. If you need the bread today set the bowl near the oven, if tomorrow is more convenient leave in a cool place overnight or for really slow raising – 48 hours – put the dough in the refrigerator. Once the loaf has doubled in bulk, quickly knock it back by punching it with your fists. Scrape it up in a lump and knead the dough on a floured working surface for 1-2 minutes.

Preheat the oven to 425°F (220°C/Gas Mark 7). To shape the cottage loaf, divide the dough into 2 pieces, one about a quarter of the size of the other. Place the smaller piece of dough on top of the larger and skewer them together by pressing the floured handle of a wooden spoon down through both pieces. Remove the spoon handle and place the loaf on a greased baking sheet. Bake for 10 minutes, then reduce the oven temperature to 375° F (190°C/Gas Mark 5) and bake for 30 minutes more.

Corn pones

Cornmeal is the basis of many endearingly countrified types of bread.

3 cups (1 lb/450 g) cornmeal

1 teaspoon baking powder

1 teaspoon salt

1 1/4 cups (1/2 pint/300 ml) milk and warm water mixed

2 tablespoons finely chopped onion (optional)

milk to glaze

Preheat the oven to 400°F (200°C/Gas Mark 6). Sift the cornmeal and baking powder into a bowl and add the salt. Gradually stir in the liquid, adding a little onion as you go. The dough should be soft but not sloppy.

Turn onto a floured surface, flour both hands and shape pieces of dough into "pones" – oblong cakes about the size of a small envelope, and 3/4 inch (2 cm) thick.

Put onto a greased baking sheet, brush the tops with milk and bake for 20-30 minutes, or until golden brown. Eat hot, dripping with butter.

Below: A home-baked Cottage loaf shares a table with a crusty brown baker's loaf and jugs of flowers picked from the local hedgerows.

Right: Gingerbread, baked in a shallow, circular shortbread mould. If you don't have a suitable mould, stamp the dough out into biscuits using decorative cutters such as those shown on p.119.

Gingerbread

More a biscuit than a bread, my version is pressed onto a mould before baking so as to impress a decorative pattern on its surface.

2/3 cup molasses (1/4 pt/150 ml black treacle)

2/3 cup (1/4 pint/150 ml) water

1/2 stick (2 oz/150 g) butter

6 tablespoons soft light brown sugar

2 1/2 cups all-purpose flour (10 oz/275 g plain flour)

2 tablespoons ground ginger

1/2 teaspoon ground cinnamon

1/2 teaspoon baking soda (bicarbonate of soda)

pinch of salt

Preheat the oven to 300°F (150°C/Gas Mark 2). In a heavy pan mix the molasses (black treacle) with the water, butter and brown sugar. Melt together over a gentle heat.

Remove from the heat and sift the flour, ginger and cinnamon into the warm, sticky mixture. Dissolve the baking soda (bicarbonate of soda) and salt in a little boiling water and add this to the mixture. Stir or rather push it around with a wooden spoon; then take over the kneading with your hands until it forms a smooth, very stiff dough. At this point add more flour if it is not stiff enough.

On a floured board roll out the dough to about 1/3 inch (8 mm) thick. Flour the dry and spotless mould then press the panel of paste firmly into it. Carefully ease the moulded dough out and onto a buttered baking sheet.

Bake it in the warm oven for 45 minutes (any hotter and the gingerbread will melt and lose the pattern). With a palette knife, transfer the gingerbread from the baking sheet to a wire rack (it will harden as it cools).

DAIRY
—DISHES—

Strawberry cream

Crushed strawberries have twice as much flavour as the whole fruit, which seem to get ruddier and more insipid every year. This recipe brings out whatever taste they have. Serves 2-3.

1½ cups quartered ripe strawberries
(8 oz/225 g ripe strawberries, quartered)
1 tablespoon sugar
juice of ½ lemon
1 envelope unflavoured gelatin (¼ oz/7 g gelatine)
2 tablespoons warm water
2 tablespoons warm milk
1 ¼ cups heavy cream (½ pint/300 ml double or whipping cream)
almond oil for greasing (optional)

Mash the strawberries, discarding any mouldy or badly bruised ones and push them through a hair sieve into a bowl. (A plastic sieve will do, but not metal.) Stir in the sugar and lemon juice.

Sprinkle the gelatin onto the warm water in a small bowl and set aside until spongy. Add the warm milk. Set the bowl over hot water and stir the gelatin until it dissolves. Strain it onto the strawberry purée. Whip the cream and stir it into the strawberry mixture.

Transfer the strawberry cream to a bowl or mould, and either keep in the refrigerator or in a cool place until needed. If you want to turn the cream out, smear the mould very thinly with flavourless oil first. Almond oil is the correct thing, but vegetable oil does just as well. Do not use olive oil, however, which has too strong a flavour.

Crowdie

Crowdie is the Scottish term for cottage cheese. This remains the best way of using up skim milk, but pasteurized whole milk can be used. The quantities given here make a small bowlful (see photograph).

5 cups (2 pints/1.1 litres) milk
2 teaspoons essence of rennet (1 teaspoon prepared rennet)
salt to taste
1-2 tablespoons half-and-half (top-of-the-milk)

Heat the milk in the saucepan until tepid. Remove from the heat and stir in the rennet, then leave in a warm place until set to a firm curd (this takes about 2 hours).

With a long-bladed knife, slice the curd across one way, then the other, to make 1-inch (2.5-cm) divisions. Spoon the cut curd over and cut the long pieces up into more cubes. (Curd cutting is routine in semi-hard and hard cheesemaking and enables whey to drain freely off the curd.)

Heat the curd in its whey gently until warm, stirring. Leave to settle for a few minutes, then turn into a muslin or cheesecloth bag and drain for a few hours. Tip the crowdie into a bowl, salt lightly and mix in the half-and-half (top-of-the-milk) to make it spread better. Store in the refrigerator – it will keep for several days.

Right: Shown from right to left, Strawberry cream, made in an antique mould and served on an Irish creamware plate, Junket (for recipe see p. 164), served in heart-shaped dishes, and Crowdie, served in a brown and cream earthenware bowl.

Junket and cream

Junket is such a simple, unpretentious dessert that it tends to be overlooked. Personally, I much prefer it to the current favourite, yogurt, especially with a little thick cream. Serves 4.

2 cups (16 fl oz/475 ml) whole milk

2-3 teaspoons sugar

2 teaspoons essence of rennet (1 teaspoon prepared rennet)

⅔ cup heavy cream (¼ pint/150 ml double cream)

grated nutmeg or ground cinnamon

Heat the milk in a saucepan over low heat until just tepid. Add sugar according to taste, stirring well. Pour into a flat dish, stir in the rennet and leave to set. Pour over cream and sprinkle with spice before serving.

Dur mou

This old French family recipe starts with a basic chocolate mousse mixture made with lots of eggs and ends up with something between a soufflé and a squidgy cake. You then sandwich a layer of the chocolate mousse mixture between two layers of the *dur mou* for an unbelievably, wickedly rich result.

11 squares dark German chocolate

(11 oz/300 g dark chocolate)

2 sticks sweet butter (8 oz/225 g unsalted butter)

1 cup (8 oz/225 g) sugar

9 egg yolks

pinch of salt

5 egg whites

Preheat the oven to 300°F (150°C/Gas Mark 2). Melt the chocolate with the butter in the top of a double boiler set over simmering water. Beat the sugar with the egg yolks until smooth. Mix this with the chocolate away from the heat, adding it gradually.

Beat the egg whites in a clean bowl with a tiny pinch of salt until stiff. Fold into the chocolate mixture gently but thoroughly. Have ready 2 oiled 7¼ inch (18 cm) cake pans. Divide about two-thirds of the cake batter between the pans and bake for 1 hour. Meanwhile, keep the remaining cake batter/mousse in the refrigerator.

Let the cake cool. Spoon the mousse over the cake base and sandwich the two halves together. Eat warm or cold.

PRESERVES

Gooseberry jam

This is one of the easiest jams to make, as gooseberries have a high pectin content and set readily. If you like a slightly tart jam, it is also one of the nicest. Unripe gooseberries are best for jam as their skins are less tough. If you can, cook the berries in a copper preserving pan so that they keep their green colour. Otherwise they will turn a pinkish-amber shade. Makes 8-10 lb (3.5-4.5 kg).

4 pounds (4 lb/1.8 kg) unripe green gooseberries, trimmed
5 cups (2 pints/1.1 litres) water
12 cups (6 lb/2.75 kg) sugar

Put the gooseberries in a large copper pan with the water and bring slowly to a boil. Mash the berries with a spoon and continue to cook for 20 minutes.

Warm the sugar in a bowl in a 275°F (140°C/Gas Mark 1) oven. Add it to the gooseberries and allow it to dissolve. Bring to a boil. Test, after 10 minutes, by dropping a little jam on a saucer and setting it in a cool place for a minute or two. The jam should wrinkle at the edges. When you run a finger through the middle of the jam, it should stay in two separate sections. It may need 15-20 minutes to reach setting point.

Blackberry cheese

This has more texture than blackberry jelly, but without the seeds that you find in blackberry jams. Dewberries or loganberries may be used instead of blackberries. Quantities will depend on the success of your gathering. As a rule of thumb, use approximately equal quantities of blackberries and cooking apples, and 1 pound or kilo of granulated sugar to each pound or kilo of pulp. Makes about 6 lb (2.8 kg).

2 pounds (2 lb/900 g) cooking apples
2 pounds (2 lb/900 g) blackberries, washed
granulated or preserving sugar (see method)

Peel but do not core the apples; cut them up roughly. Put the fruit in a saucepan with water almost to cover and cook slowly, covered, until reduced to a pulp. Rub through a coarse sieve into a bowl, adding a little more boiling water. Weigh the strained pulp and add an equal weight of granulated sugar. Stir over a gentle heat until the sugar has dissolved, then boil up to the setting point (reached very quickly), taking care that the mixture does not burn. To test for a set, see instructions given in the recipe for Gooseberry jam. Pot and seal.

Dried apricot jam

This jam can be made all-year-around as dried apricots have no season. The grapefruit supplies acid – two lemons can be substituted. These ingredients make 3 lb (1.4 kg).

2 cups (12 oz/350 g) dried apricots
7 cups (3 pints/1.75 litres) boiling water
4 cups (2 lb/900 g) sugar
juice of 1 large grapefruit or 2 lemons
2-3 tablespoons slivered almonds

Wash the apricots, put them in a large bowl and pour over the boiling water. Leave for 1-3 days, until the apricots are swollen and soft.

Turn the apricots and soaking liquid into a pan and simmer until tender. Add the sugar, grapefruit or lemon juice and almonds. Bring to a boil and boil until the jam reaches the setting point. Test, following the instructions in the recipe for Gooseberry jam. Pot, seal and cover.

Top left: Junket, sprinkled with cinnamon and served in a heart-shaped dish. Bottom left: A generous slice of Dur mou.

Right: Clockwise from top: Gooseberry jam, Lemon curd, Blackberry cheese, Dried apricot jam.

Lemon curd

Until you have tried home-made lemon curd you have no idea how good the stuff can be. Spread it on bread, or use it as a filling for a home-baked sponge cake. This makes about 1½ lb (675 g).

1 cup (8 oz/225 g) sugar lumps
2 large lemons
⅓ stick (3 oz/75 g) butter
3 eggs, beaten

Rub the sugar lumps over the lemons so that they absorb the flavoured oil from the skin. Put the sugar lumps in the top of a double boiler. Add the butter. Squeeze the juice from the lemons and add this to the pan with the beaten eggs.

Set the pan over barely simmering water and cook, stirring constantly, until the mixture thickens.

Pour into jars. When cold, store in the refrigerator.

*A selection of culinary plants, freshly picked from a
country herb garden in California. The herbs shown
are red salvia, heart's ease, nasturtium, salad burnet,
lemon verbena, sorrel, sage, tarragon and marigold
(false tarragon).*

—THE KITCHEN— GARDEN

Country kitchens furnished with bunches of herbs and strings of chillies, along with country meals cooked up from the freshest vegetables, are easier to achieve if you have a country garden outside your kitchen window, planted with beds of aromatic herbs, unusual salad vegetables and, if there is space, a fruit tree or two.

If you lack a garden, but still hanker after a little country greenery to freshen your home and flavour your food, you can compromise by lining up rows of pots brimming with herbs, or even salad stuff, on your windowsill, roof terrace or balcony.

For ease of use, a herb and produce garden should be sited as close to the kitchen as possible, so I have included some advice in this chapter on the different ways in which you can make your garden layout beautiful as well as practical.

The restoration of the famous *potager* at Villandry in France made gardeners look at vegetables with new eyes. As a result, creating a little *potager* that is visually satisfying as well as productive has become something of a cult. The fruits of the earth are mundane compared with its flowers, but healthily burgeoning and disposed in orderly *parterres* that are neatly enclosed by hedges of dwarf box, thyme, or a crisp frieze of chives or parsley, they provide a handsome as well as an appetizing show.

A *potager*-cum-herb garden can occupy a space quite close to the house, instead of

Below left: Geraniums, whose bright, edible flowers can be used to transform the plainest salad, share a sturdy terracotta pot with another useful plant for country cooks – a baby bay tree.

Below middle: The simplest – and the sweetest – strawberries you can grow are these Alpine wild fruits.

Below right: Red salvia flowers will brighten your garden and are useful in the kitchen to hot up a vinaigrette dressing.

policy is to go for food that tastes spectacularly better freshly picked, like salad materials, or that is difficult or expensive to obtain commercially, like rocket, sorrel, quinces, lovage, or that grows rampantly for very little trouble, like courgettes or alpine strawberries. Many herbs come into this latter category too; rosemary thrives, once established, sage and marjoram likewise. Summer and winter savory are pungent, sturdy little plants that should be made more use of. I bought my lovage plantlet, not believing for a moment the salesperson's prophecy that it would grow hugely tall and bushy. Like

being banished to a patch beyond the shed at the bottom of the garden. This is altogether more satisfactory because any gardener will spend more time tending a visible stretch of his or her territory and a well-tended kitchen garden will, of course, respond by producing more abundant and delicious fruit and vegetables.

The celebrated gardener and garden writer, Rosemary Verey, grows small fruit trees at focal points in her elegant *potager*, to give scale as well as fruit. Some fruit, preferably the rarer soft fruits like white or black currants, are indispensable where space

allows. The old manorial, walled kitchen gardens could afford to devote large plots of ground to the traditional soft fruits, which grow so well and with such flavoursome results, in the British climate. The walls gave support and shelter to espaliered fruit trees, while a hothouse ripened more exotic produce such as grapes and melons.

If space is the main restricting factor to your ambitions in the food-growing line, the other is time. Unlike most shrubs, which seem to require only a minimum of attention, vegetables and fruit need fairly regular upkeep. If you have limited time to spare, the sensible

angelica, a stem easily reaches 6 or 7 feet (about 2 metres), so its sharp-cut foliage and large flower heads make it a striking customer for the back of a deep bed or border. Crushed, the leaves are extremely aromatic, with a eucalyptusy sort of tang. They are good threaded onto barbecue skewers with kebabs of pork or white fish.

Quite a few of the plants I have mentioned are decorative and well-behaved enough (i.e. not too invasive and rampant, like courgettes) to be grown in and among the flowering plants and shrubs in a border. This is a popular way of growing some edible plants without going to the lengths of creating a separate, regular kitchen garden. Lack of space and time is what usually prompts this strategy, plus the feeling that if you possess only a sliver of urban garden, it is more important to grow things there for colour, scent and beauty than to supplement the greengrocer's offerings.

It is surprising how much can be packed into existing beds and borders – a clump of sorrel in a shady corner, borders of chives and parsley, alpine strawberries for ground cover, a shock of silver rosemary in full sun. Grape vines and wall-grown or standard fruit trees

Below left: Bushes of rosemary scent the air delightfully and, freshly picked, add hearty flavour to soups, stews and roasts.

Below middle: No kitchen garden should be without a few drifts of mint. This versatile herb can be used to flavour sweet and savoury dishes; as well, it has medicinal purposes.

Below right: Patches of herbs nestle together, identified by hand-cut wooden plant tags.

clumps of herbs festooned with bees and butterflies is an excellent compromise, very much in the current spirit. All that needs emphasizing, from the practical point of view, is that almost all herbs do best in full sun and well-drained soil.

For a *potager* or kitchen garden to carry conviction, and look more impressive than a simple vegetable patch, you will need to include taller elements to give it scale. One way of solving this problem is to install a central arbor, consisting of two iron arches, up which climbers can be trained. These can be grown purely for their looks, in which case

also provide something to eat as well as to look at. In fact, I often wonder why more people don't plant fruit trees, which are decorative in blossom and fruit, instead of the so-called ornamentals, which look spectacular for a week or two and then pass into insignificance. If you can only find room for one or two fruit trees, choose one of the rarer varieties that are now being assiduously re-established in more imaginative nurseries. I often regret that more people don't plant mulberry trees, however slow-growing, because this is delicious to cook with, and almost impossible to find commercially.

A small, formal herb garden is probably the most successful answer to what to make of a confined space. The recent revival of interest in knot gardens, *parterres* and other types of layout that pre-date the great romantic garden enthusiasm of the 18th century, has restored the formal garden to favour. Herbs are a natural choice to stock formal garden beds with, with their historical associations, beautiful names and scents, and pleasantly untidy habit of growth. Tidy *parterres* filled with tidy plants smacks of public parks, but neat beds edged with clipped dwarf box or lavender and filled with great drifts and

clematis, roses or wisteria would be suitable choices. Or, more appropriately, plants can be selected for their food value, in which instance runner beans or vines would be ideal as they are both fast-growing and vigorous.

Obelisk-type supports, set up in the middle of the beds but accessible by narrow brick paths, extend the idea of adding height attractively. These can be simple teepee shapes formed from a handful of bamboo stakes tied together at the top, their bases firmly pushed into the soil, or, more lavishly, they can be made of a metal or wooden

latticework, available from garden suppliers. Paving of some sort makes an immense difference to kitchen gardening, practically as well as visually, because it cuts down on the amount of mud you will carry back into the kitchen. Bricks laid herringbone-wise make traditional and pretty paths, with the advantage that, because you only need to use the weakest sand-and-mortar cement to hold them in position, the layout of the *potager* can be altered or revised without too much trouble. In fact, if you lay them into a previously dug trench, on a base of hardcore or cinders, you can pack them together so firmly that you won't need to use any cement at all.

Concrete paviours come in all sorts of colours, sizes and finishes – smooth or riven – and make a solid, practical paving whose raw colour when new soon weathers to something mellower. Lay them in combination with cobbles or brick for a more appealing effect. Gravel paths, properly laid, are probably the least expensive surfacing available and can look very attractive, and rather French, when the beds are neatly enclosed in low hedges of box or lavender.

If your new kitchen garden lacks old walls of rosy brick, it may benefit from an enclosure of a different sort that will give your plot an intimate "garden room" feeling, as well as acting as a windbreak and micro-climate for your plants. Medieval gardens were often enclosed by a wooden palisade – basically a

Left: This large Californian kitchen garden is crammed with a bumper selection of herbs – sage, chives, majoram, sorrel, parsley, chervil, thyme. The owner, Sharon Lovejoy, use her crop to flavour food or make scented teas or bath potions. Surpluses are dried to market as cooking mixtures or pot pourris.

Above: In the foreground, lemon verbena and peppermint plants feature. Behind are rosemary bushes underplanted with chives, red salvia, thyme and curry plant. The owner is careful not to mar the garden's charm with modern tools; she uses an old-fashioned wooden wheelbarrow and metal watering can.

Below: Like the owners of this picket-fenced Connecticut garden, the inhabitants of the beehive enjoy the tastes of the herb bed. As a result, the honey they produce has a flavour unmatched by commercial varieties.

waist-high fence, but more showy, painted dark green, perhaps, with gilt finials and other decorative bits and pieces. A solid fence of this sort might create too much shade in a small kitchen garden, where a trellised enclosure would be more suitable. It would still give something of the same effect if you top the upright posts with wooden balls and finials and paint the posts and trellis in an appropriate colour. The charm of this arrangement, too, is that it makes an ideal framework for training up climbers or supporting espaliered fruit trees.

A "green" fence, consisting of a row of cordon-trained fruit trees, is another possibility. This has the virtue of being highly productive, yielding its own tasty crop as well as fulfilling the requirements of shelter and enclosure. It should be said, though, that pruning is an art in itself, and one that is not easy to master, so perhaps this is not the solution for novice gardeners. Planning based on a thorough knowledge is important as different species need different pruning times, and often in different degrees – some lightly, others severely. If you can't distinguish between a fruit and a leaf bud, or you cut the wrong way, branches have an exasperating habit of going off at a tangent. However, for the persevering, neat rows of cordon or fan-trained trees make a fine sight and a fruitful addition to a *potager*.

If you can afford the space, try to make a place to sit in the sun and contemplate the coming harvest. Pave an area just large enough to take a bench and plant the beds up close to it so that the most fragrant herbs are within smelling distance. Bees and butterflies love herbs, and nothing induces a greater sense of peacefulness than drowsing on a sunny bench watching the insect world hard at work collecting honey and pollen.

Your bench doesn't have to be wooden – grassed seats are another appealing medieval

Above and right: A mixture of home-grown flavourings. Shown right, clockwise from top left: lavender heads filling a wooden bowl; cloves in a heart-shaped pottery dish; star anise in a broad-rimmed earthenware dish; cinnamon, flaked into a heart-shaped basket; cranberry sprays piled into a big wooden bowl; pepper seeds in heart-shaped white china; bay leaves in heart-shaped terracotta.

conceit. A modern version can be seen in the famous gardens at Sissinghurst Castle, England. It consists of a raised earthy platform that is hollow at the top so that the cavity can be filled with soil and planted with thyme, camomile or another tough, creeping herb which will act as a living scented pillow. The medieval versions were raised quite high, but the idea could be adapted to create something more benchlike, with a back to lean against, by building two containers to grow the plants from, one at seat height and the other a couple of feet higher.

A herb or kitchen garden mixes well with that other current craze – the wild garden. This trend has reached the more enterprising nurseries, who offer seed-grown native plants such as cowslips, bluebells, primroses and lilies of the valley, plus some rarer beauties like the bewitching snakeshead fritillary, said to grow in the water meadows around Oxford and the Isis, although I have never been lucky enough to spot one.

Though the natural habitat of such plants is quite different from the domestic garden – and difficult to recreate – there is something to be said for planting a selection of them in a special bed in a *potager* or herb garden. Here they can be properly seen and admired, as their fragility and modest colouring means that they tend to be over-looked if they are planted in a more floriferous position, among showier, cultivated blooms. Harvested, these gentle flowers are appropriate decoration for English country kitchens, particularly those in the cottage style.

DIRECTORY

KITCHEN SPECIALISTS, JOINERS, CABINETMAKERS AND DESIGNERS

GREAT BRITAIN

Mike Chalon
The Plaza
535 King's Road
London SW10
(071) 351 0008
Antique and reproduction country style furniture.

Robert Davies
11 Gun Street
London
E1 1AH
(071) 377 2030
Carving, gilding a speciality.

Kerry Edwards
11 Deal Street
London
E1 5LJ
(071) 247 3756

Tony Heaton
The Malt House
Sydney Buildings
Bath
BA2 6BZ
(0225) 466936
International interior design service.

James Howett
11 Gun Street
London E1 1AH
(071) 377 2030
Designs to commission.

Luke Hughes
1 Stukeley Street
London
WC2B 5LT
(071) 404 5995
Custom-made wooden kitchen furniture.

John Lewis of Hungerford
Park Street
Hungerford
Berkshire
(0488) 682066
Country style built-in kitchens and free-standing wooden furniture.

Hugh Lander
Brewer Farm
Lanner
Redruth
Cornwall
TR16 6BS
(0209) 217557
Historic buildings consultant: gives advice on kitchen building and design.

Alison Macdonald MCSD
27 Chalcot Square
London
NW1 8YA
(071) 722 3318
Kitchen design.

Martin Moore
28 Church Street
Altrincham
(061) 928 2643
Wooden and painted kitchens.

Newcastle Furniture Company
Green Lane Buildings
Pelaw
Tyne and Wear
NE10 0VW
(091) 438 1342
Wooden and painted kitchens.

Robinson and Cornish
The Old Tannery
Swimbridge
Devon
(0271) 830732
Wooden or hand-painted built-in kitchen furniture.

The Shaker Shop
25 Harcourt Street
London W1
Shaker-style painted wood kitchens and furniture; also baskets, peg rails, pottery, herbs, accessories.

Smallbone
Hopton Trading Estate
London Road
Devizes
Wiltshire
SN10 2EU
(0734) 591459
Handcrafted natural or painted wood kitchens in a wide selection of designs, including a freestanding (unfitted) style.

Dave Smith
Sunrise Cottage
107 Upper Cheddon
Cheddon Fitzpaine
Taunton
Somerset TA2 8LD

Mark Wilkinson
Overton House
Bromham
Chippenham
Wiltshire SN15 2HA
(0380) 850004
Wooden and painted kitchens; designs include Provençal and Santa Fe styles.

Woodstock
23 Pakenham Street
London WC1X OLB
Wooden kitchens.

FRANCE

Grange
695090 St Symphonien-sur-Coise
Period-style French, American and Shaker-style freestanding furniture.

USA

Nan Hearst
Hearst and Co. Architecture
435 Jackson Street
San Francisco, CA 94111
Architect.

Smallbone
150 East 50th Street
New York *and*
315 South Robertson
Boulevard
Los Angeles
Hand-painted and solid wooden kitchens; including a freestanding style.

POTTERY

GREAT BRITAIN AND IRELAND

Marion Brandis
9 Bloomsbury Place
Brighton
BN2 TDA
(0273) 688299
Potter.

Emma Bridgwater
Unit 0
Atalanta Works
Atalanta Street
London SW6 6TR
Decorative spongeware pottery; also glassware.

Divertimenti
45-47 Wigmore Street
London W1H 9LE
(071) 935 0689

139-141 Fulham Road
South Kensington
London SW3 6SD
(071) 581 8065
A wide range of cooking utensils and tableware.

The French Kitchen Shop
42 Westbourne Grove
London W2
(071) 221 2112
Suppliers of pottery from England, Spain and Italy. Also stocks a wide range of utensils and general kitchen equipment.

Hinchcliffe and Barber
Studio 5
Town Farm Workshop
Dean Lane
Sixpenny Handley
Salisbury
Wiltshire
(0725) 52549
Spongeware pottery and tiles; coordinating fabrics.

Isis Ceramics
Old Toffee Factory
120A Marlborough Road
Oxford
Hand-painted Delftware.

Sophie McCarthy
77A Lauriston Road
London E9
(081) 9869585
Hand-thrown jugs, platters, bowls with more than a hint of the Bloomsbury decorative manner.

David Mellor
4 Sloane Square
London SW1
Cooking utensils and tableware.

Nicky Mosse
Mosse Pottery
Bennetts Bridge
Co Kilkenny
Eire
(056) 27105
Decorated pottery, including spongeware.

Simon Pettit
13 Gibraltar Walk
London E2
(071) 2561274
Delft-style pottery to order.

Owen Thorpe
Churchstoke Pottery
Churchstoke
Powys
SY15 6AG
(0588) 620511
Potter.

Mary Wondrausch
The Pottery
Brickfields
Compton
Near Guildford
Surrey
GU3 1HZ
(0468) 4097
Hand-potted slipware. Undertakes individual commissions.

Andrew and Joanna Young
Common Farm
Sustead Rd
Lower Gresham
Norwich
NR11 8RE
(071) 2787700
Hand-potted kitchen and domestic stoneware in brown and green glazes.

FRANCE

L'Artisanie
61 rue de la Republique
92 Meudon-Val-Fleury
Pottery.

Kitchen Bazaar
6 avenue du Maire
75015 Paris
(010) (33) (1) 45 48 89 00
Classic and modern pottery and cook's tools.

Genevieve Lethu
95 rue de Rennes
75006 Paris
(010) (33) (1) 45 44 40 35
Provençal pottery. Also stocks cook's tools, fabrics, baskets and other country-style accessories.

La Tuile a Loup
35 rue Dauberton
Paris 5
(010) (33) (1) 4707 2890
Traditional pottery for the table and the kitchen from the regions of France.

USA

Bennington Potters
324 Country Street
Bennington
Vermont 05201
Traditional-style earthenware, including spatterware.

Rowe Pottery Works
404 England Street
Cambridge
W1 53523 9116
(0101) 1 800 3565003
Salt-glazed stoneware; also iron racks, pan stands and trivets and candle-holders. Mail order service available.

ANTIQUES

GREAT BRITAIN

Louie Kanz
59 Walcot Street
Bath BA1 5BG
A lively emporium filled with eccentric and decorative pieces from Europe, India and the Far East. Fabrics, furniture and accessories.

Lunn Antiques
86 New Kings Road
London SW6
Antique table linen, lace and other textiles.

Guimond Mounter
Bakers Farm
Dulford
Devon
(0884) 6358
Pine and country furniture, including primitive pieces.

Obelisk Antiques
2 Silver Street
Warminster
Wilts
BA12 8PS
(0985) 846646
Distinguished period furniture from England, Europe, USA; also prints, accessories, porcelain.

Keith Skeel Antiques
7-9 Elliott Place
London N1
Antique kitchen furniture, distinguished period furniture.

Spread Eagle Antiques
22 Nelson Rd and
8 Nevada Street,
Greenwich SE10
(071) 8589713
Antiques and pictures, distributed over two premises.

Geoffrey Stead
158 High Street
Burford
Oxfordshire
OX8 4QY
Antique dealer.

The Dining Room Shop
62-64 White Hart Lane
Barnes
London SW13
(081) 878 1020
Antique furniture, china and porcelain, table linen, kitchenalia.

Tobias and The Angel
White Hart Lane
Barnes
London SW13
Primitive furniture and kitchenalia.

Wakelin & Linfield
10 New Street
Petworth
West Sussex
(0798) 42417
Country furniture.

Robert Young Antiques
68 Battersea Bridge Road
London
SW11 3AG
(071) 2287847
Country furniture and kitchenalia.

USA

Indigo Seas
123 North Robertson
Boulevard
Los Angeles CA 90048
(0101) (213) 550 8758
Antiques; Interior design service.

Winsor Antiques
53 Sherman Street
Fairfield
CT 06430
(0101) (203) 255 0056

TILES

GREAT BRITAIN

Fired Earth
Middle Aston
Oxfordshire
OX5 3PX
(0869) 40724
Terracotta, slate and limestone floor tiles; traditional wall tiles.

FRANCE

Corema
35 quai de Pre Long
BP144
77403 Lagny
Traditional tiles.

TEXTILES

GREAT BRITAIN

Anta
46 Crispin Street
London E1
(071) 247 1634
Tartan fabrics; also tartan-patterned pottery.

Ian Mankin
109 Regents Park Road
London NW1 8UR
(071) 7220997
Natural fabrics - tickings, checks, stripes.

Souleiado
171 Fulham Road
London SW3
(071) 589 6180
Provençal print cotton fabrics, table linen, oven gloves, aprons in natural and plasticized cottons.

Les Olivades
16 Filmer Road
London SW6
(071) 386 9661
Provençal print cotton fabrics.

Un Jardin en Plus
100 Mount Street
London W1
French-made floral fabric and tablelinen. Also country furniture, pottery, accessories.

FRANCE

Ebene
38 boulevard Victor Hugo
Saint Remy-de-Provence
Provence
(010) (33) (90) 92 36 10
Authentic Provençal fabrics and furniture.

Les Olivades
1 rue de Tournon
75006 Paris
(010) (33) (1) 43 54 14 54
Provençal cotton fabrics.

Souleiado
78 rue de Siene
75006 Paris
(010) (33) (1) 43 54 15 13
Provençal cotton fabrics by the yard/metre. Table linen. Also sell wicker furniture and rush-seated chairs and settees.

Un Jardin en Plus
105 rue de Fg
St Honore
75008 Paris
(010) (33) (1) 43 25 75 98
Floral fabrics, table linen. Also country furniture, pottery, accessories.

USA

Grau
7520 Melrose Avenue
Los Angeles
CA 90046
(0101) (213) 461 4462
Fabrics, clothes and other accessories. As well as her original designs for clothes, Claudia Grau sells Central American furniture and fabrics.

Howard Kaplan's French Country Store
35 East 10th Street
New York 10003
French country fabrics, accessories, pottery.

Pierre Deux
870 Madison Avenue
New York 10021
French Provençal fabrics, faience dinnerware.

STOVES & RANGES

GREAT BRITAIN

Aga-Rayburn
Glynwed Consumer & Building Products Ltd
PO Box 30, Ketley
Telford TF1 4DD
(0952) 641100
Distributor for both Aga and Rayburn ranges.

La Cornue
60 Westbourne Grove
London W2
(071) 792 0991
French restaurant-quality stoves.

USA

Antique Stove Heaven
5414 South Western Avenue
Los Angeles CA 90026
(0101) (213) 298 5581
Reconditioned antique stoves.

Vulcan-Hart
PO Box 696
Louisville
KY 40201
(0101) (502) 778 2791
Restaurant-quality stainless-steel stoves.

FRANCE

Galerie la Cornue
Paris 75006
(010) (33) (1) 46 33 84 74
Restaurant-quality ranges.

Godin
532 rue Sadi-Carnot
02120 Guise
() (16) 23 60 41 42
Wood-burning stoves.

PAINT SUPPLIERS AND FINISHERS

GREAT BRITAIN

Nemone Burgess
49 Ledbury Road
London W11 2AA
(071) 2295498
Decorative painter.

Emma Coe
11 Gun Street
London E1 5LJ
(071) 9483391
Decorative painter.

Emma Hardy
25 Leighton Grove
London
NW5 2QP
Stencillers.

Tom Hickman
10 Bath Street
Frome
Somerset
(0373) 73076
Murals and stencils.

House Style
17a Huguenot Place
London E1 5LJ
Paintability stencils and House Style paint finish kits.

Mary McCarthy
7 Bridge Street
Stiffkey
Wells-next-the-Sea
Norfolk
NR23 1QP
Decorative painter.

Rose of Jericho
Dene Corby
Northants
NN17 3EJ
Historic paints, renders and plasters, including limewash.

USA

Pottery Barn
Williams-Sonoma
100 North Point Street
San Francisco
California
House Style paint finish kits and Paintability stencils.

CANADA

Vanessa Benitz Imports
4913 Boulevard de Maison
Neuve
Montreal
House Style paint finish kits and Paintability stencils.

HERBS, FLOWERS AND GARDEN PRODUCTS

GREAT BRITAIN

Candlesby Herbs
Cross Keys Cottage
Candlesby
Spilsby
Lincs PE23 5SF
(075) 485211

Hollington Nurseries
Woolton Hill
Newbury
Berks RG1 59X
(0635) 253908
Herbs, scented climbers, old roses, topiary. Mail order.

Iden Croft Herbs
Frittenden Road
Staplehurst
Kent TN12 ODH
(0580) 891432
Herbs, aromatic plants, demonstration gardens. Mail order.

L'Herbier de Provence
Fulham Road
London SW6
Herbs, oils, vinegars; also dried flowers.

Kaundry Farm Herbs
Nesscliffe
Shrewsbury
Shropshire SY4 1AX
Medicinal herbs a speciality; also dried arrangements.

Keepers Nursery
446 Waterinbury Road
East Malling
Maidstone
Kent ME19 6JJ
100 apple varieties, 20 pear, 30 plums. Also soft fruit. Old varieties a speciality.

Ken Muir
Honeypot Farm
Rectory Road
Weeley Heath
Clacton-on-Sea
Essex CO16 9BJ
(0255) 830181
20 varieties of strawberries, 40 of cane and bush fruits. Two varieties of asparagus.

Norfolk Lavender
Caley Hill
Heacham
Kings Lynn
Norfolk PE31 7JE
Lavender plants and products. Mail order.

Paula Pryke Flowers
210 Denton Street
London N1 9PS
'New wave' florist specializing in country style flowers, fresh and dried.

Jo Russel-Smith
Sunrise Cottage
107 Upper Cheddon
Cheddon Fitzpaine
Taunton
Somerset TA2 8LD
(0823) 451716
Dried flower arrangements.

Seeds-by-post
Suffolk Herbs
Sawyers Farm
Little Cornard
Sudbury
Suffolk CO10 0NY
Seeds for wild and cottage garden flowers, unusual vegetables.

Tolman's Nursery
Wotton Road
Ludgershall
Aylesbury
Bucks
Nursery specializing in unusual and beautiful cottage garden plants.

Ken Turner
Thomas Goode and Co.
Conduit Street
London W1
Natural flower and plant arrangements, scented candles and pot-pourris.

USA

Heart's Ease
4101 Burton Drive
Cambria CA
805 927 5224
Garden and herb shop selling baskets, wreaths, garlands, bouquets, herbs and spices, garden accessories.

FRANCE

L'Artisan Parfumeur
8 rue de la Boetie
75008 Paris
Dried flowers, candles.

ARCHITECTURAL SALVAGE

Lassco
St Michaels Church
Mark Street
London EC2
(071) 7390448

Renzland Forge
83A London Road
Copford
Nr Colchester
Essex
(0202) 210212

Walcot Reclamation
108 Walcot Street
Bath BA1 5BG
(0225) 444404

Yapton Metal Co.
Burndell Road
Yapton
Sussex BN18 0HP
(0243) 551359

ORNAMENTAL IRONWORK, FURNITURE, ACCESSORIES

Ironart
61 Walcot Street
Bath BA1 5BN
(0225) 446107

Nick Jarman
Hulshay
North Petherton
Somerset
(0278) 663490

BASKETS

USA

Shaker Workshops
P.O. Box 1028
Concord
MA 01742
Baskets in the Shaker style. Also trays, containers, boxes.

FRANCE

La Branche d'Olivier
19 rue Monge
75005 Paris
(010) (33) (1) 43 34 10 00
Baskets.

L'Artisanat
10 rue Jean-Jaures
13200 Arles
Baskets.

INDEX OF
RECIPES

—GENERAL— INDEX

ACKNOWLEDGMENTS

The Author and Publishers would like to thank the following house-owners, architects, designers, potters, herb-growers, antique dealers and museums for allowing special photography for this book:

Stephen Andrews, Jane Baijeant, Jean and Vony Becker, Mike Chalon, Liz and Jim Cherry, Colleen Covington, Jane Cumberbatch, Hannerle Dehn, Dick Dumas, Maria Luisa Larranaga Condesa Vda de Foxia, Steven and Sandra Gibbons, Claudia Grau, Nan Hearst, Tony Heaton, Tom Hickman, Hinchcliffe and Barber, Lyn and Nigel Howard, Patou von Kersting, Lyn von Kersting and Richard Irving, Wendy Kidd, Hugh Lander, Stephen and Maribelle Leavitt, John Lewis of Hungerford, Sharon Lovejoy and Jeff Prostovich, Stephen Mack, Jane and Terry Macey, Heidi and Christopher Marchant-Lane, Melanie Martin, James Merrell, Bill and Angela Page, Carol and Malcolm Parker, Jaime Parlade, Peter and Silvie Schofield, Sarah and Giuseppe Sesti, The Shaker Shop, Lars and Ursula Sjoberg, Keith Skeel, Jacqui Small, Smallbone, Susan Suchopar and Ladislav Samuels, Susan and Michael Schneidemann, Sally Spillane and Robinson Leech, Mimi and Geoffrey Stead, Anna Strasbourg, Derek and Judy Tolman, Tullie Smith Museum, Ken Turner, Andrew and Julie Wadsworth, Michael Wakelin and Helen Linfield, Mary Wondrausch, Andrew and Joanna Young, Robert and Josyane Young.

The Author would like to thank: Kate Harris for her assistance with the recipes and all at Mitchell Beazley, especially Judith More for being unfailingly helpful throughout the course of the book.

The quotation on page 79 is from Patience Gray's *Honey from a Weed*, published by Prospect Books (1986).